is the eldest of three brothers, for whose parents were both teachers. Will was distinctly average academically, he was possibly above average at sailing, but nothing else. His first job was a lowly paid position selling advertising space over the telephone. Like lots of other people, Will was working his way through life as a wage slave with a nice house, nice car and nice holidays. Then, in 1991, his life changed – Will was made redundant. He quickly went into debt and had to sell his possessions to pay his rent, including some very personal items given to him by his parents. In short, Will was forced to take stock and rethink his life.

So he did. This book is partly his story, which follows the birth of King of Shaves from a fledgling start-up to a global brand that has disrupted the market through innovation, insight, ground-shaking ideas and hard work and now competes with the $60-billion brand Goliath that is Gillette. Far more importantly though, this is a guide for budding entrepreneurs to embrace Will's ideas, to use the best of them and transform their lives both professionally and personally, in more uplifting, fulfilling ways than you can ever imagine. This is Will's story, but it could be your story too, if you're prepared to be the best you can be – a king.

Or in Will's case, the King of Shaves.

The Author

Will King was born in Lowestoft, Suffolk in August 1965. Will

THE KING OF SHAVES STORY

WILL KING

headline
business plus

First published in 2009 by
HEADLINE PUBLISHING GROUP

First published in paperback in 2010 by
HEADLINE PUBLISHING GROUP

1

Cataloguing in Publication Data is available from the British Library

ISBN 978 0 7553 1999 2

Typeset in Memento by Avon DataSet Ltd,
Bidford-on-Avon, Warwickshire

Printed and bound in Great Britain by
Clays Ltd, St Ives plc

Headline's policy is to use papers that are natural, renewable and
recyclable products and made from wood grown in sustainable forests. The
logging and manufacturing processes are expected to conform to the
environmental regulations of the country of origin.

HEADLINE PUBLISHING GROUP
An Hachette UK Company
338 Euston Road
London NW1 3BH

www.headline.co.uk
www.hachette.co.uk

Dedication

This book is dedicated to Tony and Shirley King, Mum and Dad,
for without them, there'd be no me, and definitely no
King of Shaves.

Contents

Acknowledgements

Thanks to Herbie, Ann, Suann, Andy, Pat, Antony, Doug, Brian and all our shareholders, along with the fantastic team I've had the pleasure of spending the last sixteen years alongside – Karen, Jane, Simon, Lisa, Bill, Richard, Vicky, Charlie, Yasmin and everyone else, shaving lives, one stroke at a time.
Great thanks are also due to James Wills of Watson, Little Ltd for giving me the chance to bring the King of Shaves story to a global audience. Thanks also for the huge support from my partner in helping make this book a reality.
All of you, in your own way, mean more to me than you will ever know.

22/2/92

My dear William,

It was good hearing your usual voice on the phone last night and to know that things are moving along on the Whitbread front.

I've enclosed a letter from M.S. (Martyn Styles) just as a reminder that not so long ago you were the tops – and people recognised it. (I came across it when spring cleaning and dumping over half term.) I thought that if you read it again you would have a grin and remember some very good and successful times at Cowes. It doesn't do any harm to pat oneself on the back on a job well done.

Your present predicament is only temporary and will be seen as a minor hiccup when you look back in the months ahead. Cream always rises to the top!

I enclose a cheque to cover the Walker Log plus expenses and buyers commission. I've booked my first interview with Shirl re the Early L. series on Friday. At the moment I'm hoping for a completion and launch next Autumn but... it might not be as long as it sounds. We'll have a business chat when you come down for a weekend.

I also enclose some ideas from the Observer re jobs, just as a focus for the future.

Look forward to hearing from you,

Yours ever,

  Dad

    x

Prologue

'A recession was going on.
I decided not to participate.'
Anon

November 1993

King of Shaves:	Gillette & Wilkinson Sword:
Sales: £300	Sales: $Billions
Employees: 1	Employees: Thousands
Office dogs: 2	Office dogs: 0
Note to self: 'Nothing like a challenge Will.'	

The 'how' and 'why'

Yesterday, while at my brother Doug's house for Sunday lunch, I told him and Dad that following the publication of a profile on me in *Shortlist*, the top-selling men's magazine, I'd been approached by James Wills of literary agency Watson, Little Ltd and asked to write a book about King of Shaves. They both exclaimed, 'Before it goes to the publisher, we want to read the manuscript!' When I asked why, they replied, 'Why would people be interested in reading about King of Shaves?'

They had a point. Why indeed? After all, I'm no Richard Branson, Alan Sugar or James Dyson. I'm not on *Dragons' Den*, nor am I worth hundreds of millions of pounds. I don't have a racy rags-to-riches story that will keep the reader glued to the pages, wondering how I went from zero to hero. Indeed, the King of Shaves brand is still a long way from being the global brand I believe it will be in my lifetime. In short, their point was why would anyone want to read my book?

So I thought about what they had said and about how to make my book interesting and of practical use. Simply put, I had to get across the point that success is genuinely accessible. It was a challenge to me, and the comments of my family refocused my mind on making this book immensely useful for readers considering how to determine their own destiny, as entrepreneurs or otherwise.

Well, this book is the why and the how I did it, and am doing it today. It is a book designed to give readers an insight into building a brand in the face of formidable competition – in my case Gillette and Schick-Wilkinson Sword – two businesses with a combined market capitalization of some $62 billion. These are competitors that most would view as impossible to compete with. Imagine them as rocks weighing 62 billion tons, and you can exert a force of just 1 or maybe 2 tons. How would you dislodge them, disrupt them or break them up?

This book is a hybrid. It is partly about me, concentrating on King of Shaves, with a lot of 'you can do it too' along the way. It's entirely written by me, not ghosted. If you are prepared to engage with me, what I've done along with my team and how I've done it, it may well prove to be your pass to accessing areas that have previously been closed to you. Sure, you can google stuff here and ask people questions there, but rarely will successful people (and I guess I'm now regarded as one of them) truly share with you the 'how to do it and how to get it done'. This is because in the grown-up world there is often a direct link between hatred and competitiveness, whereas as a child you are far more likely to be kindly and collaborative. Therefore, my first piece of advice is to keep an element of the child in you.

The value of kindness and collaboration

As we get older, displaying acts of kindness sometimes brings you uncomfortably close to other people. Often, being kind is viewed negatively by the person to whom you're extending your kindness. You're saying 'let me help you' and yet they may be too proud to accept your help, believing they should be able to help themselves. They wonder why you're being kind ('What's in it for you?') and sometimes question the motivation.

When you're a child, you have yet to develop the concept of distrust. This comes when you are thrust into the adult world of surviving on your own and you develop a wariness of others – a competitive, selfish streak that's 'all about you'. But, when you're a child, before your brain rewires itself, you like to play and collaborate and, often, offer genuine acts of kindness that you do not expect a reward for. This kindness often leaves many of us, resurfacing only later in life, when you feel a need to 'put back' into society.

The perhaps controversial point I want to make is this. Most people believe that to be a successful entrepreneur or businessperson you must have competitiveness and distrust or hatred in spades. Where kindness and collaboration are concerned, these are considered to be weaknesses.

Wrong.

I would argue that truly successful entrepreneurs, that is, people who are able to shape their lives and those of others for the better, value the power of kindness and collaboration. Sure, they may be competitive (in my case, I simply want to do better) and know that not everyone is going to be like them (see pages 171 and 180 to read about when I was taken for a ride by a conman who exploited my kindness), but overall, if you're going to transform your life and determine your own success, you have to get close to people, treat them as friends and embrace the notion that 'what's given out, is gotten back'.

Start planning and doing

I want to make entrepreneurial success accessible to you, not a mystery or something you can't do. Clearly, not everyone will be a success – indeed, when you read this book you'll see how many failures I went through before finding success. It's like cooking a dish for the first time, you're unlikely to come up with a Heston Blumenthal, three-Michelin-starred result first time round – far from it.

This book has been written to allow you to access success that you maybe only ever dreamt of. I'm not necessarily talking about material wealth either – few entrepreneurs set out to make loads of cash at any cost. Indeed the best, most success-ful entrepreneurs view cash generation simply as a useful by-product of doing something extremely well. No, this book is about achieving what you are capable of. In my case, my ambition was to become the 'king of shaving'. (Well – *Which?* magazine thinks we're doing a great job with our King of Shaves Azor razor, awarding it 'Best Buy' and 'Exceptional Value' in their April 2009 issue.)

Finally, you may well be reading this book while we are still in the middle of a gloomy recession. Let me tell you, this is the very best time to read it. If you can take heed of the lessons in this book, recognize who you are and what you want to be, you'll see that timing and luck is extraordinarily important in success and there is no better time to found a recession-proof business than when in the depths of a recession. After all, you don't know how high you can go until you know how low you've been.

Want longevity and success? Start planning (and doing) right now. I did, and if I can, so can you.

Will King,
April 2009

Chapter New: You

I've read dozens of business books, as diverse as Victor Kiam's *Keep Going For It* to Richard Branson's latest tome, *Business Stripped Bare*. Although they are great reads – don't get me wrong, I enjoyed them – I didn't really buy them to simply enjoy them. I bought them in the hope that reading them would help me to be successful, that I would find in their prose ideas that I could latch on to, achieve and make happen, and in doing so, turn my latent potential into tangible results.

Over the past sixteen years, I've read (and reread) two great, life-shaping books – *Maverick!* by Ricardo Semler, a book that literally shaped how I run Knowledge & Merchandising Inc. Ltd (KMI – the company that owns the *King of Shaves* brand) and *I Know It When I See It: A Modern Fable About Quality* by John Guaspari. I'll talk about their impact on me and King of Shaves in due course.

However, a lot of business books don't explain in detail how you can do it too. After all, there will probably only ever be one individual among the world's billions who will start off publishing a magazine for students and end by setting up a spaceship company, having along the way founded, among other ventures, a record label, an airline and a bank. There'll only ever be one Richard Branson.

I'm interested in *you*.

That's why this chapter isn't called chapter one, it's 'Chapter New'. Because, if you've bought this book to see how you can achieve what you want to achieve, you've made the right choice. I wanted to write this book to help you see that dreams can become reality, as long as you embrace a few key concepts along the way and observe a few rules, more of which shortly.

This book can't guarantee you success. But it can demonstrate that 'Impossible is Nothing' and 'Just Do It' (respect Nike, adidas!) are valuable ideas.

We live in a time of great uncertainty. After twenty years of growth in almost everything, the world is rebalancing. Having been violently sick in 2008, it's now hungover, listless. It wants to stay in bed, sweating out all the toxins in it, all the dodgy debt and the leveraged borrowings. But in times of great uncertainty comes great opportunity. In times of stability and comfort easy cash – the enemy of creativity – rules.

To understand what 'chapter new' means, I invite you to consider the following scenario that I found myself in. It is the situation that led me to 'chapter new' and the creation of King of Shaves.

For me 1991 looked like this: I was in full-time employment, earning £30,000 per year. I had a company credit card and company sports car. I owned a flat (albeit I was in negative equity having bought at the top of the market in summer 1988). I enjoyed great holidays, my life was on track and everything was generally great. Then, I was made redundant.

One year on, 1992 looked like this: I had no savings and moved into a rented flat. The mortgage on my previous property was not covered. I had accumulated debts of more than £10,000. I had no car, I didn't even have a bike, and no job. I had no idea what to do. I was thoroughly miserable.

This could be you. I hope it isn't, as it's certainly not a great place to be. But if it is, welcome to chapter new. You.

SPACE

It's time for you to learn about SPACE and what this acronym means. Why not make a note of it right now, as I refer to it constantly throughout this book?

S: Satisfaction of success
P: Passion and persistence
A: Attitude of action
C: Confidence and common sense
E: Enthuse, exceed, ENJOY!

Each 'letter' will be dealt with in turn, but to give you a taste, here's a bit about the satisfaction of success – the 'S' in SPACE.

The satisfaction of success

To understand what the satisfaction of success looks like, you need to know what down and out means.

Many people go through life never knowing (or understanding) the satisfaction of success. Don't get me wrong, the satisfaction of success isn't being worth tens or hundreds of millions of pounds. It's not about having the cars, the yachts, the homes (note the plurals) either. It's about something much more important than the acquisition of material things (although, if you develop a successful business, money is one of the key by-products). It's when you look at something you've done and you say to yourself 'I did that'.

The satisfaction of success for me was having the courage to take the step from doing nothing to doing something. That courage was drawn from a letter I received from my father, the one you read on page ix, which he wrote to me when I was at my lowest ebb. As I said earlier, you need a friend to succeed.

In my case, my parents were my friends. To get you going you need a friend to help show you the way because the hardest thing you're ever going to have to do if you are to succeed is to overcome inertia and develop momentum. Starting things from scratch is so hard. Starting to write this book was hard. Starting a new relationship is hard. Starting is the single hardest thing to do in the world.

Imagine you have no idea of the concept of starting something. What I mean is, there is a task to be done and you simply do it. You don't stand and look at it, worry about doing it and procrastinate over it. This is (in my opinion) where 99.9 per cent of people who could start benefiting from chapter new, don't. They turn away from the task in hand and from getting on with it. This is great news for you because it means that 99.9 per cent of your potential competitors – future business owners, entrepreneurs, etc. – are never going to go into battle against you. Imagine if everyone wanted the same job, all 6.5 billion of them. What chance would you have in getting it? One in 6.5 billion. Not great odds. But luckily, most people eschew chapter new and carry on living the same old story, even though they know how it ends.

Being a Tigger

I'm a Tigger. Let me explain what I mean.

'Excuse the boldness of my approach. I'll come straight to the point.' So opened my letter that I wrote in the late 1980s to a chap called Andy James of Digital Equipment Corporation (DEC), a massive US computer manufacturer. I had never written to him before, but I surmised that he was a busy chap and that I needed to make an impact on him and get straight to the point. Andy was the first person to call me Tigger. If you want to kill inertia and overcome the hard part of starting up, in your own way you've got to develop Tiggerish character-istics. You need a relentless, boundless optimistic enthusiasm for what can be achieved although it is yet to happen and an intoxicating blend of self-belief, confidence and 'I will get to the top of the tree even if I fall out on the way up'.

I met Andy James before I was made redundant. Andy called me Tigger because of my enthusiasm to get on to the pitch list for DEC's sales conferences and product launches. (I'll talk about what I did for a living pre-King of Shaves a little later.) The nickname Tigger was only reapplied to me in 2006, by my girlfriend while on a sailing holiday in the British Virgin Islands. She started calling me Roary Tigger, i.e. a Tigger that roars. In all that time, from 1989 to 2006, I hadn't once thought about Tigger.

What Andy and my girlfriend saw in me was a boundless enthusiasm for being supremely optimistic. This trait, above all, is the one that can overcome inertia and get the ball rolling. I bring this enthusiasm to almost everything I do. I don't do things half-heartedly. Whatever is to be done, I throw myself into getting it done, day after day after day after day. As there are 365 full days in a year, this, I can tell you, is a lot of enthusiasm and it can be pretty tiring. Don't get me wrong, I'm not some sort of crazy guy going around all the time doing everything at 200 per cent. This 'tiggering', as I call it (as defined by me in urbandictionary.com), is mainly in my mind. It keeps my brain busy. It gives me a mental momentum that is the difference between something being successful and not.

Where you're concerned, this is great news because as long as you're prepared to use your brain to think positive, bouncy and exciting thoughts, you can be a Tigger too. However, if you're an Eeyore, give up right now. Eeyores can never be

Tiggers, as much as Tiggers can never be Poohs. In fact, you must do your very best to keep Eeyores out of your life. They are not blessed with what you have and as much as you may want them to be like you – to smile, have fun and believe everything is possible – they're genetically coded to never be comfortable with this. So leave them to their own devices. This is a key point. If you've bought this book I can only guess that you want to know how to be a Tigger and to utilize that wonderful zest and vigour for life to succeed in your chosen field. What I'm going to be talking about, from pretty much here on in, takes the view that you want to be a Tigger too.

Returning to the matter of friends, since I got my Tigger nickname back I read A. A. Milne's book, *Winnie-the-Pooh*, and realized that between 1992 and 2009 I've had all of Tigger's friends around me in varying guises – wise Owl, friendly Pooh, miserable Eeyore, timid Piglet and caring Kanga. Funny that, or maybe not. Maybe all these characters are around you right now, and if you choose Owl, Pooh or Kanga rather than Eeyore, maybe you'll be on your way sooner than you think.

Find yourself a great business partner

I was lucky enough to meet a wise Owl, a chap called Herbie Dayal, a talented management consultant with an MBA from INSEAD (a top-ranked international graduate business school and research institution) and who'd worked with US consultancy Booz Allen Hamilton. You'll get to know him throughout the book. For a great business to take off it almost always involves a partnership – Bill Gates and Steve Ballmer (Microsoft), Steve Jobs and Steve Wozniak (Apple) are just two examples of great partnerships. Rarely does a business scale and globalize if it's just one person driving it; even Richard

Branson has developed plenty of Virgin partners along his route to success.

As you read this book, which is clearly written from 'my view', there is also 'his view', i.e. Herbie's, and that balanced vision is critically important for a business. So, here's Herbie talking about what's been changing in the world of work since the mid-1980s and what this may mean for you and about his experience of working with me over the past sixteen years:

> *I believe that since the beginning of the 1980s, the number of people wanting to be self-employed, rather than employees of other companies, has been growing dramatically. As the wealth of the nation has grown and as the notion of a job for life has dwindled, so more and more individuals have yearned to be in business for themselves. Their motivations are usually based on wanting to be their own boss, wanting to earn more money from what they do and having a better quality of life (no commute, see the children more, etc.).*
>
> *Many of my friends who have set up their own businesses know very well what the downsides are. You can work night and day on your business. When you are not actually working you are worrying. You can work for years (or for ever) earning a lot less than in your previous job and over time you become less and less employable. The downsides are as formidable as the potential upsides are attractive.*
>
> *Although I'd invested in KMI from the outset in*

early 1993, it wasn't until 1995 that I started working at KMI full-time. I was now working in a business that had an annual turnover that was much less than my salary from my consultancy! With a wife, home and two young children just starting school, this was not an easy time.

Getting into product was the important thing. Both Will and I had been providing services; in his case marketing events and in my case management consultancy. In service industries the client buys your time and your expertise. If you are not around (on holiday, working for another client or otherwise unavailable) you do not earn money. If you are selling a product consumers can be buying it even if they don't know you, if you are on holiday or when you are asleep. The other important motivation to get into product is that perhaps you can create a business that somebody else could buy from you, hopefully providing you with a life-changing sum of money. It is generally rarer that service businesses are bought, especially small ones that appear to rely heavily on the skills of one or two people.

Will and I worked on a number of product business ideas. What is clear is that when you have nothing then ninety-nine per cent of the ideas you come across seem pretty good! You are desperate to get into something. Now that we have a sizeable business we seem to turn away over ninety-nine per cent of the ideas that come to us.

So when Will came to me with a small bottle of shaving oil and told me it helped his razor burn and that it would maybe help others, I naturally regarded it as a possible business idea. This is despite the fact that it was a completely different technology from shaving foam, looked completely different, went under a brand name nobody had heard of and we had absolutely no money to market it. On top of that we were going to compete with one of the biggest and best-known companies in the world and we would need shelf space from the UK's biggest retailers – in which we had no contacts whatsoever. Analytically it did not stack up at all.

What did stack up was the enthusiasm and optimism Will brought with that first bottle. Having watched him work on other businesses in the past it was clear that he was a doer and that if the business failed it would not be for lack of trying.

There is a delightful childishness in being a Tigger. In the Prologue, you will recall my connection between kindness, collaboration and being a child. Tiggers are always pushing forwards, sometimes to their detriment, but often to make great discoveries and earn great rewards. But if they try and do it on their own, they'll get stuck up the tree, with nowhere to go other than to fall down. This Tigger knows how important it is to have Owl beside him.

In the hot seat

I'm sure you'll be familiar with the phenomenally successful game show, *Who Wants to be a Millionaire?* The thrust of the show is simple – answer twelve questions correctly, one after the other, and you can win £1 million. The first questions are easy but then they get harder. Along the way you get the chance to secure a prize level, but if you want to go all the way to £1 million, you have to have faith in your general knowledge and be prepared to risk all to gain great reward. Over all the series broadcast there have been a handful of one-million-pound winners but literally tens of thousands of competitors. Clearly, this isn't a reliable way to make £1 million. So, imagine you're the contestant in the hot seat. Because, if you're serious about determining your own destiny, in the way this book will outline, then that's exactly where you are – in the hot seat.

The reason I draw reference to *Who Wants to be a Millionaire?* is not for the cash sum you can win. It's about the structure of the show, the importance of having (or having access to) knowledge, the need to repeatedly gamble with your beliefs to move upwards and the way you interact with people around you – those you know (phone a friend) and those you don't (ask the audience). These are two of the three lifelines offered to contestants, which are hugely important if you're setting off to start your own business. The third lifeline, where two of the four answers are taken away, giving you a one in two chance of getting the question right, I'll come on to. When you start up it's probable that you will have a raft of ideas for your business, but at some stage, you'll have to back the right idea.

To summarize chapter new, this is a critically important point for you if you are serious about starting your own business. Chapter new literally means starting over. That is, finding a prime location to spend years digging strong foundations for you and your business and realizing the fact that there's no such thing as an overnight success; it can take five–fifteen years, or perhaps longer. It's also knowing that to achieve your goals you have to display childlike, not adult, traits that will allow you to bounce around or over obstacles placed in front of you by the herd who follow conventional thinking and are not prepared to overcome difficult challenges.

Who wants to be a millionaire? Well, I presume you do. So, let's get on with it.

Chapter 2: Finding Your Purpose

School days

Allow me to introduce you to my life, and most significantly, the moment at which it was completely transformed.

My parents, Tony and Shirley, moved to Lowestoft in the early 1960s so that Dad could take up a teaching job (as head of PE) at Alderman Woodrow Grammar School (now Kirkley High Comprehensive). Mum was a primary school teacher, initially at Meadow Primary, then at Pakefield Primary.

With Mum and Dad being teachers we had a thrifty, yet comfortable upbringing. We never wanted for much and although I guess money was always tight, my brothers and I enjoyed what would probably be viewed today as an idyllic childhood. Computer games didn't exist (although Pac-Man and Space Invaders games were highly wished-for Christmas presents) and we spent most of our time outside in the garden, on the beach or down the rec (council recreation ground).

Doug and Pete, my younger brothers, were both excellent at every ball-sport going – football, cricket – you name it, they played it for the school or at county level. I, on the other hand, was rubbish at ball-sports, but good at war games, being in the Cub Scouts and balancing on my first skateboard – the Tangerine Terror that the father of my schoolboy friend Chris Lambarth made for me using a short plank of wood and a couple of roller skates.

I distinctly remember sitting on the coal bunker in our house in Kirkley Park Road, probably aged about nine, thinking to myself (while holding my guinea pig, Wellington and rabbit, Bluebell, who we discovered later was actually a boy) that life was brilliant. Days seemed to take ages to go by, I got on well with my mum and dad, tried to hang around with my cool, athletic brothers and skateboarded, go-karted or cycled everywhere. Life *was* good, but then things changed.

I have always been quite a sensitive chap and take things to heart easily. Indeed, even now when people e-mail me with what I regard as strong criticism of my company's products, I take this personally, often far more than I need to. I don't know why – neither of my brothers particularly has this trait of sensitivity – but I am sometimes moved easily to tears.

Anyway, in the mid-1970s the educational landscape was being rewritten somewhat and I was knocked for six having to go to a new middle school in Pakefield, South Lowestoft. This was a new school and we were to be the first intake, in effect skipping a year at Meadow Primary, spending three years at Pakefield before going on to the now Kirkley High School (KHS) where Dad taught.

'Bender King'

I *hated* Pakefield Middle. It was big, it was impersonal, the quality of teaching was very average and it had no history and no soul. It had (in my mind, anyway) some seriously thuggish kids as pupils, whose names I can recount today with a slight judder. I took a bit of a beating at Pakefield Middle. Many of the kids there had elder siblings at KHS, knew of my dad, didn't necessarily like him and took it out on me, verbally and physically. Being called 'Bender King' sent a shiver down my spine. It didn't help that I was quite a naïve kid. I thought most people were kind, but soon learned that where the playground was concerned, they weren't. Fights, dead legs and threats were plentiful for me. I had a few friends, who I'm in touch with today (in fact one is a shareholder) but for the most part I was a bit of a loner. I felt that I didn't fit in, as I couldn't tell jokes and was rubbish at football, rugby and cricket, always being the last to be picked.

I wasn't that bright either. Sure, I was probably in the upper 25 per cent in terms of effort, but attainment was always a challenge, and I sometimes let my creative side run amok. I remember once writing a story about a motorbike racer called Alberto Balsam, who lived in Welwyn Garden City. I got very low marks for this work! Even worse, my maths was poor. I struggled with the simplest stuff; long division, multiplication and fractions especially, and still do today, even though I try to help my nine-year-old son with his maths homework. I quickly found myself streamed into Miss Revell's class for rejects. Maths was made even more difficult and confusing for me when I read that in Europe (with the advent of decimalization) commas instead of decimal points were used when writing numbers. In one maths exam, I got zero out of fifteen because every point was a comma (even though I think most of the sums were right). So when I came to move to Kirkley High in the late 1970s I was already struggling.

At KHS it got even worse. The kids were nastier (I was followed home by kids cracking bike chains behind my back, shouting 'jump Bender, jump'), the teachers were great in some cases, awful in others and worst of all my dad taught there as head of PE and the new-fangled department of health (i.e. sex) education.

Lunchtimes were generally spent closeted away in Dad's VW Campervan, eating my packed lunch and listening to Radio 1's Newsbeat. I typically walked to and from school on my own or got a lift with Dad. Sometimes, when I couldn't take the bullying or name-calling, I used to have a shower in the morning and hit my forehead against the bathroom wall to try and give myself a headache so I could stay at home. But, in the end, I always went to school, never got a detention, worked hard and managed to get six O levels in English language, English literature, maths, chemistry, geography and physics, although I had to resit maths as I got a 'D' the first time. I went on to study for my A levels. For a short time I was studying four subjects – maths, physics, geography and economics, but I dropped economics.

So, mine was probably a pretty average educational picture. Everything was good with my life outside of school, although I wished I wasn't always put in goal down the Walmer Road rec.

What's my passion?

After enduring the interminable piano lessons with Mrs Larsen (which I was rubbish at), the weekends would normally revolve around sport or being outdoors. As you will have gathered, I was hopeless at ball-sports, to the extent that Doug and Pete were much closer as siblings than I was to either of them. I pretty much used to just tag along unless I was out skateboarding or go-karting on my own.

Dad, being a sportsman and heading up PE at Kirkley High School, often got us access to the school gym at weekends, where Doug and Pete could play five-a-side and I'd roller skate. But I didn't have a passion – the love of something that I *had* to do everyday, week in, week out. Doug and Pete had started golfing at Rookery Park Golf Club, and as you can imagine, I was even worse at this than football! I caddied for my dad a couple of times, but it was truly awful and I hated it. I hated the fact that I couldn't play golf and hated that I was caddying. In fact, I still hate golf now, so don't expect me to do deals on the golf course!

However, Dad was a bit of an all-rounder. As well as being a single-digit handicap golfer, he was also a member of Southwold Sea Sailing Club (SSSC), where in the past he'd sailed a high-performance dinghy called an Osprey. When I was about five years old, I remember Doug, Pete and I used to get in the back of Mum and Dad's white Ford Thames van (covered with blue paint on the inside) and we were driven to SSSC to either collect or drop off Dad. However, in the early 1970s Dad had to have an operation on a slipped (prolapsed) disc that required him to wear a full-torso plaster cast for what seemed like for ever. He was incapacitated for months and this put paid to his sailing for some time.

Fizzy Wizzy

In 1978 or thereabouts, Dad saw that I was becoming increasingly left behind by my brothers and suggested I go sailing with him as his back had improved. Dad had the opportunity to buy a wooden Enterprise dinghy, sail number 14049, called *Fizzy Wizzy*, which had been owned by a couple at the school, Ben and Veronica Falat. They were top dinghy sailors and I think wanted to move on to a more high-performance dinghy like a Fireball, so *Fizzy Wizzy* was for sale. She was kept at school, upturned in one of the storage areas under a green tarpaulin, and one day Dad took me to see her. We bought her soon afterwards.

Having helped Dad finish painting, varnishing, restoring and polishing *Fizzy Wizzy* until she shone, we took her to Southwold for a sail one windy Saturday. Neither Doug or Pete were there, it was just me and my dad. Despite capsizing in the middle of the fast-flowing river within seconds of setting off, we got her righted (don't ask me how) and set off through the harbour entrance, into the blustery, cold North Sea. In that instant my life changed for ever, it gained a purpose. I had found something I enjoyed, my first flush of the satisfaction of success.

I guess I should have been scared, as most people are when they sail and capsize for the first time, but I wasn't. Maybe it was the trust I had in Dad or the fact that I seemed to be pretty good at sailing; balancing the boat against the wind by sitting out. I was exhilarated by the feeling of the spray on my face and the wind in my hair. It was a truly enjoyable, memorable experience and best of all, I appeared to be good at it!

From thereon in, I started to worry less about what went on at school and more about going sailing at every possible opportunity. I became a member of the Waveney and Oulton Broad Yacht Club (WOBYC) and crewed for anyone who'd have me, picking up my sailing expertise in Enterprises, Fireballs or Merlin Rockets – finely balanced dinghies that were difficult to sail well, yet supremely rewarding if you managed to do so.

Chris Lambarth's father had bought a Ranger dinghy that he kept at WOBYC and we went out adventuring in it. We went up into Oulton Broads – not exactly *Swallows and Amazons* but in truth, not far off. Dad offered to keep *Fizzy Wizzy* at WOBYC rather than Southwold and within a short period of time, probably less than a year and a half, I was competently helming and racing her on Saturday afternoons and Sunday mornings in the Club series. I never won, as I still had a lack of confidence in myself, but I was pretty useful.

Adventure on the high seas

In 1980 having just turned fifteen, another event occurred that further shaped my life. A very good dinghy sailor called Eric

Twiname died and as a memorial to him an event supported by the Eric Twiname Trust was established (they still have events today). This was a chance to go to the National Sailing Centre (NSC) in Cowes, which at that time was the UK's centre of excellence for sailing, and take part in a week's race training aboard their 36-foot racing yacht, *Halcyon.*

Sitting with my dad, I penned my application – I wrote about why I had started sailing, how I'd progressed and why I thought inclusion in this event would be fantastic. I sent it off. And I was one of the youngsters selected!

The event was to be held in autumn half-term, just a few weeks away. I couldn't wait. The night before going I remember I stayed up late, packing and repacking my bag. I'd never, ever been away on my own before – what an adventure.

The next day, weighed down with my red, aluminium-framed rucksack, I set off to Cowes. I had to navigate my way across London on the Underground, catch the train to Southampton and then take the Red Funnel ferry.

I remember walking from the train station in Southampton to the ferry terminal to save money. Mum and Dad had warned me about 'protecting myself' when out sailing, and I'd always suffered from chapped lips, so I remember buying Labello, a lip balm. I can recall the smell now and always associate that smell with going to Cowes.

The week was a revelation. Having walked to the NSC, about a mile and a half from Cowes town centre, on arrival I was asked to dump my kit and get changed double quick. I was then taken in a rigid inflatable boat (RIB) by a chap called Rod Carr (then the chief sailing instructor at the NSC, now the director general of the Royal Yachting Association (RYA)) to meet the Stephen Jones-designed, 36-foot yacht *Halcyon.* Helmed by Eddie Warwick (my first hero), it was powering eastwards down the Solent, under spinnaker, just off the Shrape, near Cowes.

'Get on, Willie,' Rod shouted, elegantly positioning the RIB just behind the yacht as she surfed downwind at about 10 knots. 'Jump.' So I did, and my life was transformed.

Chapter 3: The Satisfaction of Success

Why you need SPACE

Acronyms are pretty useful things for abbreviating complex ideas into something more easily digestible. KISS is one of my favourites. It stands for 'Keep it simple, stupid' and is frequently used by salespeople; i.e. if the customer doesn't understand what *it* is, they won't buy into *it*. Bill Clinton famously adapted this to great effect, with his phrase 'It's the economy, stupid'. Another acronym is DIPADA (define, identify, prove, acquire, desire, action) – a sales strategy to help you close deals.

The 'S' in my SPACE acronym stands for the 'satisfaction of success'. You will note from the preceding chapter how my life turned on a sixpence when I realized I was good at something and enjoyed the satisfaction that brought with it. So, why is it important that your life is peppered with the satisfaction of success? Well, think back to when you were a child, doing your homework or playing a sport. What you really wanted above all was the praise heaped on you when you'd got your maths homework right or scored (or been part of scoring) a goal and being on the winning side. Being praised is something that every kid (that I know, anyway) seeks and it is the very bedrock of determining how successful you will be. Sadly, many kids don't have the family infrastructure that affords them this praise, especially if they are socially disadvantaged. This is why youth clubs' involvement in group activities where praise can be given are so critically important, yet they are sadly under-recognized in today's competitive, dog-eat-dog world of school league tables and the pursuit of financial success. Praise for yourself and that afforded you, is key.

My first experience of the satisfaction of success was being selected on the Eric Twiname sailing event. Up until that time I had not regarded myself as successful at anything. Yes, I was quite a good sailor, I worked hard and I did what Mum and Dad asked me to do, most of the time, but I didn't have a great deal to show for it. Where sailing was concerned, although I had ability, I didn't win races and therefore didn't get praise for being 'Will the winner'. That's not to say I felt undervalued, I didn't, but I hadn't really taken life into my own hands and determined how it should be. The sailing event at Cowes changed that.

It's important that through your adult life, as often as possible, you feel the warm feeling of the satisfaction of success. If you're a salaried wage slave it's often hard to get traction with the idea of regular satisfaction of success. Your performance (and therefore pay – the most common arbiter of success) is likely to be reviewed once or twice a year at most. You'll probably be working in an environment (especially when you're starting out) where you struggle to influence how things could be done better.

As you get older, and if you haven't managed to work your way up through the organization as you'd hoped, you become subject to politics, agendas and the behaviour of others. Simply put, the older you get, the harder it becomes to feel the satisfaction of success. Worse still, you start to avoid risk because your mind is conditioned that way. Very few successful entrepreneurs, by this I mean of the Bill Gates or Steve Jobs level, start in their middle age. This isn't to say you can't, of course you can, and I hope my 'SPACE' analogy will show you how you can, but your desire to take risks when you are aged forty with three young kids and a mortgage to pay is a million miles from someone in their mid-twenties, with no kids and no real commitments. By rewarding yourself through experiencing the satisfaction of success on a regular basis you'll come to understand how truly pleasurable success is! And you'll want more of it. It can become a self-fulfilling prophecy.

I will go to the gym and work off the extra pounds . . .
I will reward myself for working out at the gym with a nice meal with my partner . . .
I will get back into playing sports because I'm feeling fitter . . .
I feel more satisfied with the success of the team who often lost until I got involved . . .
I want to feel this satisfaction when at work . . .
I don't, and I'm going to do something about it.

And on it goes.

If you go through life *never* knowing what the satisfaction of success feels like, then you're doing yourself a huge disservice. However, enjoying it requires willpower, motivation and hard work. Think about this while I explain the second part of my life before the King of Shaves story starts in earnest.

On the right tack

Where my sailing was concerned, from the moment I jumped aboard *Halcyon* I never looked back. I was good enough to qualify for the annual National School Sailing Association (NSSA) High Flyers course. It was held every Easter at the NSC, organized by a couple of great teachers by the names of

Martyn Styles and Frank Catt of Kent Schools Sailing Association. The kids on this course had the potential to be world- or Olympic-class sailors. As pleased as I was to get invited on this course, I knew from the first year, 1981, that I was miles off the pace in terms of my ability to become a top-class dinghy sailor. However, it became apparent that I was very good at teaching sailing.

I managed to become the UK's youngest-ever qualified sailing instructor. I took the course with people like John Derbyshire (then a sailing instructor, now performance director for the RYA and Olympic squad), Rob Andrews (also an Olympic-level coach) and James Stephens (RYA Cruising director). Who could have guessed that my fellow sailing students on that course would now be in charge of the Olympic success that sailing has enjoyed since 1996? From this I went on to run courses at the NSC (I actually *ran them*, aged seventeen). The biggest course I ran was for my school, which my dad and the then headmaster Jack Walmsley came on. It had forty kids on it and I was the course leader. I was great at it. And I loved it. The problem was, it didn't pay very well and my school days were coming to an end . . . what to do?

While teaching sailing for Suffolk Schools in Oulton Broad, I'd taught a doctor from New Zealand to sail. He wondered if during my gap year I might like to spend six months in New Zealand, from October 1983 to February 1984. Clearly this sounded fantastic, and through my teaching success at the NSC I was also able to get a seasonal instructor job, from March 1984 until my degree course started in October 1984.

By this time, I'd managed to make a bit of a name for myself through my sailing exploits. I'd won the highly competitive 1983 NSSA Regatta at Pitsford reservoir in the Laser class (thanks to Sam Cole, who generously lent me his Laser), won the Single-handed Mount Haes Trophy and won the inaugural Windsurfing Regatta. (I'd first got into windsurfing in 1981 when it was starting to take off in the UK and taught myself.) I discovered there was a course called Ship Science and Yacht Design at Southampton University, so I went for the interview in January 1983 (I stayed in Cowes of course) and managed to get myself on the course. All I needed to get were two Bs and a C in my A levels.

I got my A-level grades on my birthday, 18 August 1983. I knew even before opening the envelope that I'd not got the grades I needed. For some reason, when in the examination room I always panicked and lost sight of all the hard work I had been doing up until the point of the exam. Even now, I'm extremely reluctant to take exams as for some reason (unless they involve sailing) I flunk them. My grades were a C and two Es. Torrents of tears followed and the situation was made worse by the fact that I was running a sailing course at the NSC and couldn't take myself off somewhere to lick my wounds.

As I'd turned eighteen that day, and after getting over the shock, I took my mates to The Woodvale (Woody) pub in Gurnard and had my first ever legal drink. A lot of my fellow sailing instructors were really supportive and told me I'd get on to another course, but as I didn't want to resit (and go through the stress of another term or two of school) nor miss my fabulous gap year, I cast around hurriedly via UCAS for a similar course. That's how I ended up being interviewed at Portsmouth Polytechnic for a degree in naval architecture (which while I was away in New Zealand was changed to an honours degree in mechanical engineering). I got on to the course, in the 1984 intake, and breathed a sigh of relief, despite knowing the maths would be hugely difficult and that this was one of the hardest degrees you could undertake.

So, having led Suffolk Schools to victory in the Team Racing Championships at Farmoor Reservoir, Oxford as team manager, off I went to New Zealand. I enjoyed a fabulous, carefree time there, although I managed my finances extremely badly and had to be bailed out for a few hundred quid by my parents. I returned to the NSC for a fantastic spring and summer teaching sailing on the Solent. I sailed, I lived, I loved, I laughed – it was absolutely the best time of my life, with the anticipation of new challenges approaching.

Life at college

Starting at Portsmouth Polytechnic was a real shock. As I'd taken a gap year I was a year older than my peers and was wiser, cooler and more mature, in my opinion anyway. I got on with hardly anyone on my course, with the exception of a couple of guys – James Brind, whose sister Bryony was a prima ballerina and Patrick (Pat) Maris, who worked on the oil rigs in the summer. Both seemed more mature than the rest, maybe through their families' work or exposure to celebrity, but they were pretty much my main friends.

In January 1985 I wasn't enjoying poly at all. The maths was hard, we only had one free afternoon a week and all I seemed to be doing was working. My friends in Cowes were building Simon Le Bon's new ocean-racing yacht, *Drum*, at Vision Yachts in Cowes, and I convinced myself that jacking in the degree and jumping aboard *Drum* was a way out. I got over to Vision Yachts on a Friday in January, went to the boatyard and asked to join the build team. 'Speak to Skip,' one of my friends said, 'I think he's still looking for people to work on the team.'

I called Skip Novak straightaway, only to be told that 'Had you called earlier in the week, there could have been a slot for you.' 'Shit,' I thought to myself. Even more depressed, I rang up Keith Jackson, a sailing friend who lived on the Isle of Wight, and holed up with him over the weekend, before returning to Portsmouth on the Monday to resume my degree-course hell.

However, as the course developed I started to believe I would earn a degree and never having been a quitter, I stuck it out. During this time I engineered a lasting legacy at Portsmouth Poly, regarding the sailing club. The sailing club was one of *the* most popular clubs at university. It had the coolest people in it, held the best discos and events, attracted the best-looking girls and was always in competition with the rugby club for top club awards. In the first year, although I joined the club I rarely went there due to the fact it was run as an exclusive club for the few, where you were either in with the 'in crowd' or not. The club had quite a big budget, given it had to buy sailing dinghies, finance rescue boats and put on sailing courses, but truth be told it did little of this. This seriously annoyed me, as I felt the club was not being run in the best interests of its members.

A coup d'état

At the start of the autumn term in 1985 I decided to put a stop to it. I had a lot of friends by now throughout the sailing club and had tried (unsuccessfully) to move the thrust away from racing to training. So, I plotted a coup whereby the normal voting in of the commodore, secretary, etc., which was regarded as a shoo-in, was completely capsized. I turned up at the AGM with probably a hundred or so members who voted the *entire* committee out and put in a brand *new* committee. I was under pressure to be the commodore, but didn't want the job as that looked to be too self-serving, so I helped a very fair chap get elected to the post and agreed to head up sail training.

From thereon in, the club went from strength to strength. The elitism was completely removed and the club democratized. Lots of training sessions involving many hundreds of students were put on, the club budget was increased by the polytechnic directly as a result of what the club was doing and social events and membership continued to improve. By the end of my final year, 1987, I left with the sailing club in great shape, with new boats and regular, subsidized training weeks at the NSC.

To cap it all, I managed to come fifth in the 1987 British University Sailing Association (BUSA) Nationals in Plymouth, crewed by my on-off trainee-architect girlfriend, Faith Beckingham.

The need for change

The business lessons I learnt from all this were that you need to appeal to the many not the few to stand a chance of success, and from a company structure perspective, in my opinion it's important that the company structure is as flat, interactive and mutually rewarding as possible. I enjoyed a huge satisfaction of success in completely altering the dynamic of the sailing club to the advantage of many, many people, disrupting the elitism of the club and making its facilities available to many more people. While I had the satisfaction of success of passing my BEng (Hons) Mechanical Engineering degree with a very average 2.2, much of what I took away from poly was how I could derive satisfaction from changing the way things were done, for the better.

To this day I look at pretty much everything that KMI, King

of Shaves or I am doing and ask 'can it be better?' and 'should it be changed?' Often, the answer is 'no', it would just be change for change's sake, but sometimes this relentless questioning – 'are we good enough?' and 'is it good enough?' – pays huge dividends, when out of the questioning come unexpectedly creative solutions.

Chapter 4: Passion and Persistence

Getting off the payroll

Travelling to Lowestoft in August 1987 for my twenty-first birthday party (I had convinced Mum and Dad to let me hold it at their house while they were in France on holiday) I bumped into my parents at Liverpool Street Station. They were en route to Waterloo. The conversation went something like this:

Hi Will, what are you doing here?
I'm off to the Toft, for my twenty-first – remember?
Oh yes, well, look after the house, won't you? And, by the way, when we get back, we want you off our payroll.

And they walked on.

I guess this was the first time that I needed to give serious thought to what I would do as an adult. As much as I loved sailing every day and everything that went with it, I believed it was a young man's game (even though I was not yet twenty-one!) and unless I could somehow be a top yachtsman there was no real future in it for me. I was also pretty burned out at this stage, by teaching sailing week in, week out and partying hard. I was shortly to disgrace myself more than a little bit after drinking sixteen double vodkas at an end-of-season party, resulting in me having to write a letter of apology to Brian Cole, the then NSC boss.

Anyhow, plenty of people turned up for my twenty-first, including Faith (my now on more than off girlfriend), and along with my brothers we enjoyed a rambunctious time, dipping people upside down in a dustbin full of punch, making holes in the garage roof with sticks (being used as guitars) and generally laying good, honest youthful waste to Mum and Dad's house. It was all cleared up by the time they returned, apart from the holes in the garage roof, which I blame Pete for not sorting out!

After the party my thoughts returned to what I might do to earn a living. I knew I'd struggle in an engineering job (despite having a degree), but through my sailing I had developed a confidence in my abilities, maybe a little bit beyond my years. Given I had first gone to the NSC as a naïve teenager, I'd now matured into someone who was able to manage people aged from thirteen to sixty-five effectively and was well regarded for it. I didn't have a swollen head, but I did think 'I'm alright, I am'. This was a far cry from what I had thought of myself when I was at school!

Being teachers, Mum and Dad read the *Guardian* and the *Observer*, and while leafing through the *Guardian* I came across the media appointments section. I vaguely knew what this meant – jobs to do with magazines, maybe TV, advertising and the like, and one ad for a company called Graduate Appointments (a recruitment agency) caught my eye:

Earn £12K OTE. Call us for an interview.

I didn't know what 'OTE' meant (I subsequently learnt that it means on target earnings) but I dialled the number and was passed to a lady who proceeded to ask me quite difficult questions: 'Why was I calling? Why would I be good at selling advertising? What would I see as my strongest quality?'

When faced with a barrage of questions, rather than clamming up and humbly putting down the phone, I gave my answers and asked more questions: 'I don't know what OTE means, but I want to find out – what does it mean? I believe I'd be great at selling stuff, what do you need me to sell? When can I show you I'd be good at it?' And for the final question, about my strongest quality, I quickly replied, 'Persistence. Now, when can I come up?'

By spooky coincidence, the lady had taken a call earlier in the day from one of my sailing friends. Sarah (I think her name was) said, 'We've already got someone else coming from Lowestoft and don't really have time for another.'

I retorted, 'If I can be there on Monday, you'll meet me and not want to meet them!' She laughed, there was a pause and she told me to be at their offices on Monday at 9.30 a.m. So I was. I did well in the agency interview, well enough to take her out for drinks that evening in Fulham (I had quickly arranged to stay at my friend Pat's parents' house in London).

It turned out my job interview was with Haymarket Publishing, Michael Heseltine's publishing company, in Teddington. When I turned up, I was met with twenty to thirty other 'Young Turks' who all thought they were the business, and many of them seemed to know a lot more about the job than me (it was basically telesales for Autocar magazine). The interview process was my first initiation into the competitive commercial world. We all had to sit in a circle and one after another explain why we would be 'so much better for the position' than everyone else. I kid you not, fights broke out between interviewees. I remember one was between two friends from the same university, who basically started insulting each other and ended up having a fight!

Somehow, don't ask me how, I was asked to stay behind after the others had left and was offered a job on *Autocar*. However, as I didn't particularly have any desire to work for a magazine about cars, I asked what else was available. As you can imagine, this wasn't exactly the response they'd hoped for. I added that I didn't want to work in Teddington, I wanted to work in London. The recruiter said that there was a position open for a display sales executive for *Marketing* magazine, based in Lancaster Gate, and if I got myself there the next day I could interview for that. So I did and I got it, but not before asking the publishing director, a chap called Mike Orlov, how much money he earned (£29,000) and how long it might take me to earn the same! Mike rose to be a senior commercial figure in the newspaper industry. I think he liked my somewhat direct approach.

I had to start work the following Monday, so rushed back to Lowestoft, got hold of my girlfriend on the phone, told her I'd got a job (coincidentally she was to study the next phase of her architecture degree at the Polytechnic of Central London) and somehow we managed to rent a room in a house in Tooting Broadway, near the Northern Line. I was off!

The importance of passion and persistence

My job entailed making cold-calls to managers in business that might be interested in promoting their product or service in *Marketing* magazine. It taught me the importance of passion and persistence. As anyone who has worked in this industry will tell you, it's repetitive, hard and challenging work. I'm sure the last thing on the minds of people who ran marketing companies was taking a call from an enthusiastic young man who attempted to use his sales strategy – DIPADA (define, identify, prove, acquire, desire, action) – to get them to part with their cash for a blank piece of paper with no promise of any sort of reward. But, as I had no experience of what doing this would be like and the young members of the team – Paul

Adrian, Chris Smith, John McLoughlin and Victoria Damment – working for *Marketing* seemed pretty cool, I just got on with it. I knew that to make my sales numbers (and achieve my OTE) I had to make over two hundred calls a day, because of these two hundred, ten would take the call and maybe two would be seriously interested in booking an ad or a series of ads. So, I listened to what I was told, tailored it to suit me and hit the phones!

Paul Adrian, who now owns his own agency, Wonderwall, had been asked to mentor me, and recalls:

I first met Will at Marketing *magazine in 1987. I can still remember his curly blond hair, infectious smile, shaving rash and bad dress sense – yellow shirt to match his hair, chinos and blue blazer. The rest of us were clad in double-breasted suits! We hit it off immediately and I had the task of mentoring Will in the dark arts of selling white advertising space, starting him off on the hardest section of all – Hats, Bags, Balloons and Whistles! All under the watchful eye of Annie Swift. We became fast friends and Will was always a great laugh as we rode the last waves of the eighties advertising boom, hitting our targets by hook or by crook every week!*

Very quickly I found that the job didn't suit a lot of people and that many people would be there one week, gone the next. But our happy team of four or five telesales guys quickly established a work ethic that delivered results and started to lead to us being headhunted out of Haymarket.

If you display a passion for something and a persistence that gets it done, you're a very valuable person (VVP). Losing heart and giving up is the easiest thing in the world to do – pull a sickie, go back to bed and hide under the duvet. But trust me, if you're going to be responsible for other people's destinies (as so many entrepreneurs are) then you have to make sure you're working to your maximum capacity and capability. People who are passionate – whether it's about life, sport or work – are the people I love being around. And if that passion is combined with a persistence that means they claw their way to the top of the tree, then that is a compelling combin-ation. Once you've tasted the satisfaction of success I can guarantee you more of the same if you are passionately persistent about what you do; if you smile while you're doing it; if you exhort others to help you (and them) achieve goals (in our case, group advertising targets); if you will yourself on, making that 'one last call' dozens of times over, just in case 'this call's the one'.

But what you must never do is be stupidly persistent or move from passion to evangelism, not unless you're Steve Jobs. There is a fine line between loving what you do and wanting to share your love of that with others, and becoming truly annoying by trying to convert people to your cause. Treading this fine line between sharing your enthusiasm and preaching is one that needs constant finessing. Even now, I'm described as overzealous and evangelical about King of Shaves; what it has done, can do and will do. I have to remind myself it's only shaving. It's not solving the Middle East peace problem!

Being passionately persistent and good at your job will also mean you get singled out as a star and start to be treated like one. This often doesn't go down well with workmates or more senior colleagues, i.e. your boss. For example, while at Haymarket I managed to get an issue closed right at the last minute with an advert that came out of a company who rarely advertised with *Marketing* (they normally went with *Marketing Week*) and this company was normally only spoken to by our ad manager. Anyhow, the group ad manager (a lady called Annie Swift, very much my mentor and now CEO of the Institute of Sales Promotion) took me out for lunch (!), bought some red wine (!!) and talked about my career and how my success might affect other people. The following week, relations started to sour between our team and our ad manager.

Managing the dynamics of a pressured sales environment to achieve optimum success is a topic in itself, but suffice to say, once the manager loses the team's confidence and the desire to work harder, for longer, then it's difficult for them to regain it. This was the beginning of the end for our group and within a matter of months (I was the first or second to leave) we'd been headhunted to join new companies. Chris went to trade for the stockbroking firm Barclays deZoete Wedd, Paul went to top sales promotion agency Francis Killingbeck Bain and I joined CIL, a conference and event production company as business development executive. But this was not before a final display of passion and persistence from me.

Going out with a bang

The most significant issues of *Marketing* were the conferences and exhibitions issues, normally out in October and January, to tie in with the conference season. Having been headhunted to join a new company in February 1988, I was intent on going out with a bang! I'd been in regular contact with a chap called

Trevor McCarthy at the QE2 Conference Centre in London, which had recently opened, and managed to secure a meeting with him to present what *Marketing* could offer. *Marketing Week* was also pitching to him and this was my first head to head battle to secure what could be a really big piece of business. So, although I was about to leave *Marketing*, I hadn't let slip that I would be starting a new job, on double the salary, with a company car. I was intent on landing this piece of business for Annie and to prove to my ad manager that I could sell and close a big deal.

I set up the final presentation meeting with Trevor at the QE2 Centre, to be told that my presentation had swung it and that he would be booking a series of ads worth around £20,000. This was a *huge* amount, the average ad sold was £300–500 and here I was with a signed order for £20,000! Trevor and I had lunch, I got drunk and arrived back at the office at about 3.30 p.m. As I walked nonchalantly into the office my ad manager went crazy, questioning where I'd been, why I wasn't working and sounding off at me in front of everyone in the room.

A silence fell.

I pulled the signed order out of my pocket, gave it to her and said, 'I'm resigning. Here's an order for twenty thousand pounds. Bye everyone – see you in the pub!' I walked out to a spontaneous round of applause from my colleagues. I said some things to her that I guess I now regret, but I was twenty-one, had closed a huge deal and had the satisfaction of leaving a job where I'd probably made them five to seven times what I'd cost them in just a few months, only to be told off by my boss. You've got to earn respect, not expect it.

Annie Swift and I are good friends today. She's been kind enough to write this about her recollection of working with me:

I first met Will when I interviewed him for a media sales job at Haymarket Publishing. In rushed this fresh-faced, wide-eyed and bushy-tailed young fellow with a beam as wide as the Mersey Tunnel. After the pleasantries were over, I asked him why on earth he wanted to enter the heady world of sales. Fifteen minutes later, and seemingly without pausing for breath, he'd bowled me over and he started soon afterwards. He lapped up his training and, ever conscious of his sometimes leaning towards verbosity, was soon selling advertising space as though it was going out of fashion. His persistence and refusal to take no for an answer, combined with his indubitable charm, soon meant that he was outselling most of his team members. He was, and still is, ferociously ambitious and I knew it was going to take everything in my power to hang on to him. Sadly for me, but gladly for him, his clients were soon offering him jobs and one was just too good to refuse. And the rest, as they say, is history. Eventually I went on to publish Marketing Week *and Will soon started to appear in its pages, having literally launched King of Shaves in his garage. He founded that company with a great idea, no money to speak of, but with his usual drive and refusal to be overshadowed by the big boys. This entrepreneurial philosophy has stood him in good stead and will, I know, continue to do so.*

The crucial first step

Had I not been told to get off the parental payroll I almost certainly would not be doing what I am doing now. I had to be told to do something and having been told it, by people I love and respect, I did it. Had I not bumped into Mum and Dad that day at Liverpool Street Station I would have gaily carried on to Lowestoft, enjoyed a party and wondered what to do. Unless you have a very clear sense of *what* you want to do, then it's often very hard to get on the first rung to somewhere. In my opinion, it doesn't really matter what that first rung is. It's the first step you take that's critically important to give your life momentum. There are no room for passengers in today's ultra-competitive environment, so you either start and don't stop, or you don't start at all. As much as I'd like to think I'd be a success anyway, I needed to be told to get on with the next phase of my life. You should ask yourself, 'He did it, why can't I?'

Of course, it's easy to say. But the companies of the future grow from the planting of one tiny seed and unless I plant that seed in your head and tell you to 'get off the payroll' you'll forever be a wage slave, accepting what comes your way. That's what many millions of people are happy doing, and as long as they enjoy (or tolerate) their work, and are in work, that's fine. But I'm guessing that if you've made it this far into this book you're not happy being a wage slave and you're looking to take that first step on your own path, rather than the well-trodden one of others. Displaying passion and persistence for what you do doesn't always come easy. It's hard always being up, not down and believing that if you keep on calling, keep on pitching, keep on going that you will get your just reward. Maybe you won't. But you'll stand a much better chance of experiencing the satisfaction of success the more you work at it! Just don't push it too far and ram yourself down someone's throat day after day. There's a balance to be struck, that gets you what you want and others what they desire.

Chapter 5: Action, Confidence and Common Sense

Setting some goals

For some reason, when I started work on *Marketing* I said to myself good goals would be to:

1. Double my salary in a year
2. Get a company car
3. Own a flat

By 19 August 1988 I'd achieved these three things. I hadn't really set out to earn 'loadsamoney', but I had settled on three challenges, which at the start appeared wholly unattainable, but within a year had been achieved. There was a huge satisfaction of success for me in doing so. I'd accepted the job at CIL, which came with a car (a bright red VW Scirocco GT no less), without having passed my driving test (which I luckily passed just prior to joining!). From setting my initial goals, to earning good money and having independence, I guess I just carried on setting myself challenges and worked hard to achieve. Despite having won some good business for my new company, they didn't appear to be on the soundest of commercial footings and although I had great respect and fondness for the founder and her financial director, I felt that my career was a bit unsteady, especially as the chill winds of the early 1990s' recession were just starting to blow. However, work was still out there and I felt that my skills would be better exploited with a company that had more chance of getting on to blue-chip company pitch lists for major product launches, conferences and events. In spring

1989 I left to join a company called Hedges Wright Creative (HWC), the London-based creative division of the Hedges Wright Group PLC, an exhibition and marketing services company based in Swindon.

Joining HWC as business development manager on a salary of £23,000 and a Peugeot 205 GTi as my company car, I reckoned I had the world at my feet. Aged just twenty-five, I'd managed to haul myself up to owning an architecturally refurbished three-bedroom flat in Streatham and had a new car, I was earning a substantial double-digit income (probably more than either of my parents had ever earned) and was working with one of London's most creative production houses, with clients like Braun, Duracell, Colt Cars and the Prince's Trust. I quickly progressed to the role of business development director, having pulled in some big-grossing corporate video work from an insurance company and became one of the triumvirate running the business, alongside the creative director, Gregg and his production director, David.

Times were good. And then they changed. Just like that. Over.

All good things . . .

Many of you reading this book may not recall how quickly the UK went from boom to bust in the early 1990s. It happened pretty darn quickly, maybe not quite as quickly as the recession we're currently in, but nonetheless consumer confidence disappeared from the high street in a matter of months. Having bought my flat in Streatham at the very height of the market, I was soon paying 13 per cent interest on my £68,875 mortgage, which was about 80 per cent of my income. My girlfriend was studying and therefore not generating any income (I think her parents may have helped us out, but I can't be sure). House prices collapsed (my flat was valued at £49,995 within two years of buying it), businesses went bankrupt, unemployment skyrocketed and I just kept on working hard, pulling in business when it was there to be pulled in. Then, one day, it stopped.

What happens in recessions is what I call 'whale companies' stop spending and attempt to survive at all costs. They live off their stored fat. This means that the many 'fish' that feed off the 'whale', i.e. small supply businesses like ours, suddenly go from a healthy order book, six months out, to literally nothing at all. Companies delay or cancel product launches, sales conferences and corporate videos. They lockdown into survival mode (some cash-rich companies use times of recession to expand, but this is a different subject that I'll touch on later in the book) and for the small fry, unless they can rebase their business, it's game over. It was game over at Hedges Wright Creative. The company had recently been acquired by Mosaic Investments plc, for £7 million, in a piece of disastrously bad timing. Sales at HWC were haemorrhaging and profits had slid quickly into losses. Based in London, we weren't privy to exactly what was, or wasn't, going on at the HQ in Swindon but you didn't have to be a rocket scientist to work out that things were bad.

The company had over-expanded, had an absolutely huge fleet of company cars and needed to slash costs. As all this was happening, the founder of the London office, Gregg, decided to leave, and somehow or other I went from being the business development director to the managing director at twenty-six years of age. For a while we managed to keep afloat, but it was incredibly difficult. I rebranded the division as Fountainhead

Communications, taking the name from Ayn Rand's seminal book *The Fountainhead*. I was forced to fire some people (including the girlfriend of one of my good friends) and make others redundant (including David, the guy who had hired me, who was in his mid-forties and had a couple of kids at school), while I attempted to stave off the inevitable. Even with my average maths skills, I could work out that no revenue was coming in but lots of costs were pouring out. Even though it was a sinking ship, I believed if we could sell our way out of our predicament, we might be able to save people's jobs, and keep going. Cue Paul Adrian again:

In the early days of his career Will was always ringing me up and trying to get me to join wherever he was working. I remember one call in the early 1990s when Will was working at Hedges Wright Creative. The call would invariably always start:

'PA – it's Will King.' (In the tone of someone who was the CEO of a multinational – that was obviously to come later!) 'PA,' he continued, 'there's a role waiting for a great salesman like you here!'

It did not seem to matter to Will that I was quite happy with my own career trajectory as he proceeded to rattle out the company package and benefits! Finally, when I managed to get a word in and speak I told him I was quite happy where I was. A few weeks later Will called again to tell me that Hedges had gone into administration and he was now redundant! Coincidentally, years later Will told me that the management consultant who had closed the place down was none other than his future business partner, Herbie Dayal.

Meeting Herbie

Mosaic had hired a firm of consultants to carry out an analysis of their acquisition and clearly it was pretty ugly. In spring 1991 the company was in meltdown and I had the task of explaining to two consultants, Herbie Dyal and Tim McDowall, the position HWC/Fountainhead was in. It didn't take long for them to realize that the business had to be closed and I distinctly remember asking Herbie (now my business partner) 'Is it all over?' I did so over the phone, standing in the AV area behind the boardroom, knowing what his response would be.

'Yes Will, I suggest you look for a new job.'

Over the course of the next few weeks I carried out the process of making people redundant, finally making myself redundant one Friday afternoon in late autumn/early winter. Having alarmed the building, I put the keys back through the door (including my company car keys) looked upwards (the building was on the third floor in a nice cobbled courtyard) and thought 'That's that then.' I walked over the road to the Legless Ladder pub, ordered myself a Guinness, took out a smoke and sat there, slightly bemused. While I was in the pub, sinking my Guinness, my mood as black as the pint I was drinking, I noticed an old chap, all on his own in the corner. He was unkempt, looked unloved and extremely sad. Don't ask me why, but I went over and sat next to him and asked if he was all right. 'Not really,' he said, 'my wife's kicked me out, I've got no job and nowhere to go.' To say there was a bond between

THE KING OF SHAVES

us is probably overstating it, but at that moment I felt I had a comrade, someone who was in a worse position than me (I hadn't been kicked out by the girlfriend!) and someone who put my troubles into perspective.

Seeing life in perspective

After buying a few rounds I offered to help him get back together with his wife – not my best idea ever – and took him off into the council estate behind Battersea High Road. After knocking on the door, a huge barrage of swearing ensued from inside, ending with the words 'you'll never see me again' or something equally terminal. He was sobbing, so I took him back on to the high street, hailed a cab and asked for us to be taken to a homeless person's shelter between Balham and Tooting Bec. On arrival, I took him inside and asked that he be allowed to stay there for the night. Luckily, the person on duty agreed that he could sleep in the reception area. As I left I thought to myself, 'I will never, ever get as low as that poor chap.' I walked home.

In a book like this it's almost impossible to get into the detail that is necessary to explain why things happen the way they do. While my career had been on the slide at HWC/ Fountainhead I'd run into problems with my girlfriend, to the extent we were most often not on speaking terms. I met a new girlfriend through one of my brothers, held down some ad hoc sales consultancy work, rapidly burned through what little savings I had and had my youngest brother, Pete, living with me (with Mum and Dad helping towards his rent). I had gone from driving a top-end BMW 325i and earning £25,000 a year to borrowing my mum's X-reg red Citroen 2CV. The new girlfriend had seen a life of glitzy product launches, dinners and events evaporate to nothing and along with it, my confidence and self-belief. Needless to say, things weren't great in autumn 1991.

The attitude of action

So, let's talk about the 'attitude of action'. It would have been easy to return to Lowestoft with my tail between my legs, move back into my parents' house and think about how I was going to rebuild my life. However, what work had taught me was that to succeed, you had to have the attitude of action, a belief that if you got on with it then something would happen. Retrenching, hitting the reset button and wondering what to do simply doesn't cut it. If you're faced with challenges, work out how you're going to get around them. If there are hurdles, clamber over them or jump them. If people are repeatedly saying 'no' to your request, view 'no' as a delayed 'yes' and work out how you can change their point of view to embrace what you are trying to achieve. The trait of simply getting on with changing a situation to your advantage is a very powerful one. It aligns neatly with passion and persistence but is fundamentally about adopting a can-do, will-do attitude. Balanced against this must be the 'C' in SPACE, confidence and common sense, which I will come to later.

First, I must mention the feelings I had after leaving HWC/ Fountainhead. The primary feeling was one of anger. The secondary feeling was one of being a small fish. I was angry with the management of HWC because of my redundancy. Despite this, I had become quite close with Geoff Hedges, the chairman and founder of HWC. He and I got on well, and I think he saw in me a zest for life and enjoyment that he must have had when setting up his business.

Alongside the HWC team, I'd brought some really interesting business into the group, including big events for Visionhire, General Accident, Duracell (my last project was launching a Duracell battery at Brocket Hall, with Nick Ross, the TV presenter). I gained a certain notoriety for the off-the-wall projects the business had pitched for, including an idea for the Rumbelows Monster Sale, which involved creating a mechanical Loch Ness monster. I was angry that Geoff, in my opinion, had let me down (and, of course, the other employees) and that he'd sold the business as a going concern, knowing that its value would plummet.

I touched on the 'whale' and 'small fish' point earlier. Our business depended 100 per cent on the spend of a few, very big clients. When they spent, we delivered great profits; when they stopped, we went bust. I decided if I ever founded a business (goodness knows doing what) I'd want it to be a 'whale' business, i.e. a belt-and-braces business, with levels of protection and 'fat' that might allow it to ride out tough times. I would also want to make or sell something that physically existed, that you could touch. Having witnessed the decimation of the UK manufacturing industry during the 1980s, I guess I simply wanted Great Britain to make 'great product' and have a business that sold millions of items each year.

The value of confidence and common sense
Taking 'common sense' first, this is a hugely undervalued, under-rated term. Where business is concerned it is the quality by which you'll be judged. Look at what has happened to the world in the current recession. Did you believe that every day, year after year, we were all going to get richer, that credit would always be easy to come by and that your house would

always increase in value? Like everyone out there, I bet you did. After all, everyone else did, and if everyone 'believes' then surely the fairytale will have a happy ending?

Sadly, life isn't like this. The global economy is a closed system (i.e. everything within it must balance) and it doesn't like imbalance one little bit. Imbalance is what caused the global economy to explode from the inside out: the imbalance of lending to people who borrowed beyond their means; the imbalance of ever-increasing commodities production in the belief that consumers would always buy what was produced; the imbalance of the greater fool theory: 'I'm a fool for investing in this business, but there's a greater fool who'll buy it from me out there.' As we all know now, the world was bingeing on the credit equivalent of fast food and not following a sensible balanced diet of spend and save. It was spend, spend, spend.

I must admit, pretty early on the recession became a talking point for me with my friends, as it seemed common sense had been completely forgotten about. Everyone believed what they were told, that things would perhaps slow down because markets have a way of rebalancing themselves.

The day Lehman Brothers went down, was the day that common sense re-entered the world's collective consciousness, but sadly confidence committed suicide. From following a confident herd mentality everyone, from sophisticated city slickers to the average Joe, collectively lost their confidence and started to panic. There's little point explaining the world's financial projectile vomit of 2008 here – many others will no doubt do it far better – but it was all to do with massive global imbalance. As I said, we live in a closed economic system where every action has an equal and opposite reaction. There's no way around it. Like it or not, bingeing on six-times salary multiplier mortgages, 125 per cent loan-to-value mortgages and easy credit for everything is storing up a huge, insurmountable problem. Debt has to be paid back and if assets are worthless, the world is bankrupt.

Anyhow, I digress. The point I want to make is if you're able to combine confidence with common sense, you'll go far. It's important for people to believe in you and people like those that are confident. Whether they're quietly confident or outrageously, almost arrogantly so, assured people have a manner that is intoxicating. People want to believe that a little bit of that confidence will rub off on them. Confidence, however, often breeds complacency, or in its worst form, arrogance, so it's important that it is countered by common sense. A regular dose of common sense will do you wonders. You can cut through the bullshit with it in meetings or use it to identify the true worth of an idea or project before you get too carried away.

Somehow, all the confidence I'd gained up to the point I was made redundant hadn't been combined with common sense. I had leveraged in order to afford my flat. I spent, rather than saved. I risked a lot and when push came to shove, my only safety net were the friends around me and my parents. My confidence had gone from zero to a hundred and back again in just a few short years. So, while my confidence was low, it was time to rediscover common sense.

Cue the letter from my dad, of 22 February 1992 (see page ix).

I remember reading Dad's letter sitting in my small bedroom at 252a Elgin Avenue, Maida Vale, a room rented to me by a young woman called Ceri, now my brother Doug's long-term partner. I met Ceri through my other brother, Pete, who worked for her in Total Quality Management for Trafalgar

House, the engineering and construction company. She needed a lodger and I needed somewhere to live, having rented out my flat as I couldn't afford to live in it. So I moved in and through selling some personal possessions, made the rental payments each month.

I was in quite a state. I felt let down and disenfranchised. Almost all of my friends were doing well, holding down good jobs and, in some cases, starting to marry and have kids. There was huge social unrest at the time and, unemployment was very high. I had an idea for the Labour Party and trade unions called Workback 2000, whereby the nearly three million unemployed would each put £1 a week into a kitty and raise a fighting fund that they would use in some clever, disruptive way against John Major's Conservative government of the day. I used to spend hours writing it up, in a way that made sense to me, maybe it made sense to others, but truth be told I just needed to get my mind busy again.

The search for a job

Since leaving HWC I'd become friendly with Herbie, the consultant who'd told me I would be made redundant. For several months I hung around his small offices at 80 Fleet Street and tried to see if I could make some money being a consultant. One of my ideas – Chronicle Organisation Ltd – was an employee communications company that regularly polled employees (as a company's most important asset) to try and find out how they could work better, be happier or provide management with valuable feedback. I called this polling product the Employee Attitude Research System (EARS). At that stage, it was paper-based, pretty complex to administer and the many companies we presented it to nodded kindly, then showed us the door. It's important to remember all this was pretty much pre-e-mail, pre-internet, indeed, had timing and technology been different, this could well be the business I now run!

Faced with irregular ad-hoc sales consultancy work or hanging around Herbie's offices, I was (although you may not have guessed it) despairing of my ability to be a success. I'd come so far in such a short time and to fall so quickly was tough. As resilient and self-believing as I was, day after day of nothing was mentally and physically debilitating. I didn't exercise much, I smoked a lot of Marlboro Reds and spun my wheels.

In June 1992 I took a telephone call from a headhunter, asking me if I was interested in joining a chap I knew from my previous life and heading up the marketing communications division of a company called Convergence Group Ltd. As you can imagine, I jumped at the chance (although my previous history with him was more down than up) and quickly accepted a job as managing director of a marketing and communications company, on a basic salary of £40,000 and a TVR S3 sports car.

Once again, common sense went out of the window as new-found confidence blew right in. The job looked simply too good to be true; a start-up with funds, the ability to hire and fire, put on conferences, pitch for sales events and run product launches with almost unlimited resources.

But it *was* too good to be true. Neither I nor my senior managers in the business could make any sense of the company, its finances, its profitability or cashflow. While we all had access to our own accounts, the master account was controlled by the founder and money flew in and out of it willy-nilly. One of the company's big projects was the UK version of the Oktoberfest, put on in Battersea Park in October 1992. My mind boggled when we came into the office over the weekend, to find the company boss in his office (actually a bedroom, but that's another story) counting thousands and thousands and thousands of pounds. To say it was a surreal environment was an understatement. However, I managed to hire some pretty good talent, particularly a chap called Richard Taylor, who went on to be successful in marketing for Anheuser-Busch and Egg.

Pretty soon though, the cracks started to show and one day, while in discussion with Brian MacLaurin (then running the publicity division of Convergence prior to founding MacLaurin Communications, more of which shortly) the boss burst into my office and accused me of hacking into the company's computer system so I could see what people earned. It was a wild, ridiculous accusation. All that concerned me was what was coming in cash-wise to replace what was so obviously flowing out, and I told him I was 'resigning on principle'. His anger turned to tears, and in his office he implored me not to go, that 'everything will fall apart without you around'. Complete rubbish of course, as it was already game over. For the second time in two years I returned my company car keys and left the building.

Chapter 6:
The Eureka
Moment

January 2009

Ambergris Cay, Turks and Caicos Islands,

British West Indies

___

It's the day after Barack Obama was inaugurated as president of the United States. I've spent the last two days on this delightful private island, as my girlfriend and I are being shown plots of land by an enthusiastic real-estate agent. Plots range from $1–6 million, and that's before you build a house! Matt, the young salesman, displays the sense of enthusiasm for his job (essentially selling dreams on commission) that I had in 1992, and still have today. He's at the start of his business career, and during the tour of the island I briefly explained my SPACE acronym, which I think he partly took in; although he enjoyed his sail with me in a Hobie Cat in the afternoon more I think, realizing that often closing a sale is about timing as much as anything. In the end, we decided not to invest.

It was November 1992 and I was gainfully unemployed again. My personal life was in tatters, I had made many silly mistakes and was now back at square one all over again. Five years after starting off, I had nothing to show for my endeavours. I owned a flat in negative equity that I couldn't afford to live in and a growing feeling that I was living on other people's goodwill. As usual, I had lots of ideas, but nothing concrete. All in all, I would say I was probably at my lowest ebb in December 1992. Then, as so often happens, a confluence of events occured to change the direction of my life.

The first steps into business

I'd gone into Herbie's offices and spent the day mulling over what I could do next. He offered to drop me back home and while driving I glanced at the back seat of his car and saw a couple of printed T-shirts. Reaching backwards to grab them, I asked what they were. 'Oh,' he said, 'it's a US T-shirt brand called Animal Republic Survival Gear [ARSG]. A friend of mine who works for Lee Cooper was asked if he was interested in distributing them in the UK, but wasn't and left them with me.'

The T-shirts were good quality and their unique selling proposition (USP) turned out to be that the founder, Fred Gilbert, had developed a screen-printing process that allowed the design and texture of animals' skins to be applied to cotton, so you could wear the hide or skin of a wild animal such as a rhino, tiger, elephant or bear. I thought that was pretty cool and discussed with Herbie how we might get in contact with Fred.

Later that week (and remember this is pre-e-mail) we sent off a fax to ARSG in Los Angeles, requesting further information about the product line and whether the rights to market it in the UK were available. Fred got back in touch with us and explained that an Italy-based agent had the European rights and that we should get in touch with a chap called Gunther, who was based in a small town near the Italian Alps.

We made contact with Gunther, who spoke good English, and he agreed to meet us in London to discuss selling the ARSG line in the UK. Gunther explained that his company, Sportswear SARL, held the UK rights, but we could take them if we were able to raise orders of £10,000 or so.

There appeared to be little risk. We would need to buy a sample range of the collection, for something in the region of £500, and put it into a catalogue for presentations to retailers. The range had been presented in the US, initially to zoos and wildlife parks, and was apparently going into the trendy LA fashion retailer Fred Segal.

After transferring the money to ARSG, some weeks later a couple of big cardboard boxes of T-shirts and accessories arrived. Through some contacts I managed to pull together half a dozen young people who agreed to model the range, including Herbie's daughter Emmy, then just over a year old. Other models included an attractive PR executive I'd met in the last few months and another young woman I'd met while living in Maida Vale. We did the shoot for about £250 or so, working with a photographer friend of my girlfriend's, whose friend also styled the shoot. Within a couple of weeks we had what I thought was a fashion brand concept and presentation that might allow us to sell some product.

I then hit the phones, setting up meetings with large UK retailers such as Debenhams and Harrods, as well as with the buyers at London Zoo and Whipsnade Zoo. As I had no idea how selling clothing worked, I just got on with arranging the presentations, showing the merchandise and explaining the story behind the range. To my total surprise, a great many of the retailers were interested in taking the range, and not just taking it, but getting seriously behind it, especially Debenhams.

Within a month to six weeks we had amassed potential orders of approximately $100,000 – a *huge* amount. 'We're on our way,' I thought to myself, as we prepared the order to be faxed through to Fred. We needed to work out how we could afford to buy in the stock, as neither Herbie nor I had access to that sort of money, and things like letters of credit were unknown to me. All I knew was that retailers were prepared to buy the range and I needed to sell it to them!

We faxed the order to Fred and eagerly awaited his response. And waited. And waited. A week or so following the fax, we called his office in LA, but no one answered the phone. We called Gunther in Italy, who agreed to see what the problem was, murmuring ominously (it sounded to me) that 'Fred was a little bit like a faulty light bulb, he goes on and he goes off.'

Gunther called back within a couple of days and was extremely embarrassed. He explained that Fred had received our order and that it had 'freaked him out' to the extent that he was unable to supply any merchandise and could not do business with us. We were obviously angry (rightly so) about this. Gunther said he would try and make this up to us (Herbie and I had now spent £2–3,000 on the project) and would get back to us with a couple of other opportunities he had the rights to.

A week or so later we met Gunther in London. He said that the deal with ARSG 'was not going to happen' but would we be interested in working with Skechers, a new US footwear brand or Body Glove, a US surfwear brand that was featuring on *Baywatch*, the famous US TV show starring David Hasselhoff and Pamela Anderson. As we knew nothing about footwear we passed on the Skechers opportunity (this is now a huge US brand, with outlets worldwide – oh well!) but as I was a keen windsurfer I knew all about Body Glove surfwear and wetsuits. I couldn't believe that this Hermosa Beach, California company was prepared to do business with Herbie and me, but I knew how popular the Quiksilver and O'Neill surfwear brands were and thought there should be no reason why Body Glove couldn't also become a big business in the UK. Like O'Neill, Body Glove was best known for making wetsuits – the Pacific Ocean off the coast of California is quite chilly – and the wetsuits were to be made under licence by a Plymouth-based company called Sola. We were to have the fashion rights (T-shirts, board shorts, etc.).

Gunther explained that the European rights to the brand were to be held under a master licence by a Netherlands-based company, and that we would have the UK rights. It all seemed somewhat complex to me, especially as Holland wasn't exactly known for its surf culture, but again, what did we have to lose? Gunther arranged for us to meet the executives of the Dutch company, and in early 1993 we flew to Holland.

Without going into the to-ing and fro-ing that was involved, within a matter of weeks we had agreed to purchase two sample collections of the clothing range (which was to be made under licence in Holland) and upon payment for these (a cost of probably £2–3,000) we would have the rights to sell the range in the UK for spring/summer 1993.

You may wonder when I'm going to start the King of Shaves story. Well, all that has gone on before is an important precursor to why, alongside Body Glove, I founded KMI, the company that came to own the King of Shaves brand. With Body Glove, as with King of Shaves later on, I seized upon an opportunity and set out to make the most of it. Some opportunities lead to new ones, while other opportunities turn out to be dead-ends. There is never a clear-cut route to success. Life is about learning and everything you do, whether you realize it or not, you gain from.

The turning point

Shaving had always been a pain for me. I went through puberty relatively late and suffered from what I remember as being sore, painful acne. I used lots of medicated face washes to try and ease the problem and when I started shaving, my stubble growth was pretty sparse and irregular. When I was a teenager I had very blond, curly hair, and with my sailing, my skin took a bit of a battering. My dad bought me a Hitachi foil electric razor for a Christmas present, which I used only when I had to as it made my skin raw and itchy, and to be honest, I hated it. In fact, I hated shaving full stop.

When I started work at Haymarket I had to wear a shirt and tie, and my neck always got red and itchy. I couldn't wait to take them off at the end of the day, and every day I suffered when shaving.

My complaining about shaving became a regular morning rant. My girlfriend (who was Afro-Caribbean and therefore prone to dry skin) suggested I use some of her bath oil to shave with. Aromatherapy was starting to become quite big business in the early 1990s. It was a bit New Age but was developing a niche, with brands like Tisserand and what Anita Roddick was doing with The Body Shop. I put some of her bath oil on my face under my shaving foam. The razor I used at the time was a twin-blade, wire-bound Wilkinson Sword Protector. Now, there's a lot of my knowledge about shaving to come, but let me tell you three things: firstly, I had a pain-free shave, a total 'eureka' moment; secondly, the oil gummed the razor blades up a bit, which meant I spent half my time knocking the razor head against the sink to dislodge the sticky, oily stubble; thirdly, upon emptying the sink, an oily film was left around the edge, which (being a bloke) I left there, only to be castigated by my house-proud girlfriend. Unbeknown to me at the time, I had just enjoyed the first ever King of Shaves.

So now I had two business opportunities that needed running. One looked like it had everything going for it, it was a well-known brand name, it was a product that people knew and understood and I had goods to sell. The other was an idea for a shaving oil, not yet made, and with a million obstacles to overcome before it became a reality. The shaving market was a business that I had absolutely no background in and no access to knowledge of. I had no idea who could even make an oil that would perform like the bath oil. Added to which, it would be a business with competitors such as Gillette and Wilkinson Sword. However, the oil delivered a result that worked for me and transformed shaving pain into pleasure, so surely it was a product that others would want to use?

Not one, but two businesses

Herbie was continuing to run his management consultancy with two partners, Andrew and Patrick, and had recently secured a major contract with Kodak to open a photo portrait company in the UK called Smile. This was a joint venture with Kodak. They were putting in money and equipment, while Herbie and his partners were responsible for setting up the studio and marketing the concept. Herbie had his hands full, and with a young family had little time to help me run two companies. All I asked of Herbie was that I could speak to him on the phone when I needed to. I needed funding, so decided to work to get more investors involved in the core business, Body Glove, and established a separate business for the shaving oil. I've never shirked hard work, so, I started putting one foot in front of the other and set up two separate limited companies, with shareholders and financing.

As it was just me working from home (my girlfriend worked as a contractor in IT with Shell in London, leaving early in the morning and returning quite late in the evening), I decided I needed a friend, so bought a dog. While I was growing up we had a wire-hair fox terrier called Moke (which I largely took care of, as my brothers had little interest in dog-walking and clearing up dog mess), so I set out to buy Moke 2 – a fox terrier pup who could be my friend and keep me from working twenty-four seven.

When I went with my girlfriend in early 1993 to collect Moke, I was taken with another pup in the litter, the runt, called Dudley, who looked sad and forlorn. Although I had no money, I paid £300 on my credit card to buy Dudley as well as Moke and made the journey home, with my girlfriend rolling her eyes at having two dogs rather than one! So, I now had two companies, two dogs, one bedroom in a semi-detached house in South Ruislip to work from and no money, for either business. Best change that, I thought.

As I didn't really need to raise a lot of money for the Body Glove business until it was time to buy the clothing that I was yet to sell (!), I put that company and its requirements to the back of my mind and concentrated on the shaving-oil business.

One step at a time

How *do* you make a shaving oil?

It's important to remember that in early 1993, we had none of the information and knowledge-gathering infrastructure that we have today, courtesy of Google and the internet. Fax was the quickest (and only) way of transmitting and receiving rapid written communication, and many companies would only meet potential suppliers after receiving documentation that contained background to the product, the marketing plans for it and a lot more. I had none of this.

I had a Windows PC running at 16 megahertz with a 25-megabyte hard drive, that my girlfriend used to do her programming on; I had a dot matrix printer; and I had a (quite clever) computer programme called WinFax PRO, which allowed you to type a document and then fax it from the computer. Windows as a serious software platform was still extremely new and expensive (and I didn't have access to it) so I used a software suite called Smartware.

The biggest advantage I had, sitting in my little northwest-facing bedroom, with no room to swing a dog in (let alone two dogs), was that I could touch-type. It was my dad who had made me attend a touch-typing course. I don't know why he thought it would be a good skill, after all, secretaries were pretty much the only people who would need to type without looking at the keys. I took the fifteen-week Scheidegger course at the local Women's Institute Hall in Kirkley, aged fourteen or fifteen. Having been rubbish at the piano I expected to be terrible at learning to type as well, but somehow I picked it up pretty easily. It meant I could write letters and draft presentations very quickly.

So, this was my daily routine: get up, walk the dogs, sometimes drop my girlfriend at the Underground station, work in the bedroom from 9.30 a.m. to 12.30 p.m., walk the dogs for an hour, work again from 1.30 p.m. to 6 p.m., watch the news, pick up my girlfriend at around 7.30 p.m., have something to eat, walk the dogs again, go to bed. That was it.

Things took ages to get going. When I say ages, I mean ages. Nowadays, you can use the internet to access a huge amount of data quickly, get hold of e-mail addresses for buyers, research markets and requirements and generally compress a huge amount of work into a very short time. In 1993 I had to ring 192 to get the telephone number for Boots' head office. I would then call, only to be told I had to write to the buyer and 'no, we don't give out names of buyers over the telephone'. Letters then had to be written, on a computer running only a little faster than a snail, printed on a printer that took ages to print, then a stamped letter had to be posted (I had a good half an hour walk to the post office in Ruislip, as I had no car) and then I had to wait at least a week, or sometimes a month, before I had any reply.

With the shaving-oil business, one of my first brainwaves (or what I thought was a brainwave) was to write to the chief executive officer (CEO) of a company called Creighton's Naturally PLC, a big supplier to the fast-growing Body Shop. They were based near Littlehampton in West Sussex. I managed to get hold of the name of their CEO, a man called Gerry Clements, and wrote a letter asking him to help me develop the 'Kings Shave System shaving oil into a substantial business'. (See page 100 for an explanation of the evolution of the brand name.) Another brainwave I had was to write to Marks & Spencer (M&S) to see if a great British retailer might sell my shaving oil. I heard nothing from either, ever. I had no product and I had no money. It wasn't exactly a stellar start. So, fed up with waiting for retailers to reply to me, for some reason I started writing a novel! I could touch-type and I had the time. I could only call Boots or Harrods or M&S once a week or so to see if they would meet me to discuss my 'shaving revolution' and there's only so much time I could spend walking the dogs.

As well as writing the synopsis and opening chapters for *We Three Kings* (the first of a trilogy, the second novel would be titled *Gold, Frankincense and Murder*, the third novel *Wise Men Don't Lie*) I also started to think about the shaving-oil company doing more than just selling, well, shaving oil. I came up with a name for the company, Knowledge Merchants International (KMI), and produced my first newsletter to send out to prospective investors (i.e. Mum and Dad, Herbie and other people I knew). I still have this first issue of *The Knowledge*. As well as the opportunities with Kings shaving oil and Body Glove surfwear, was the phonetics-based reading and writing system developed by my mum, Shirley, Shirley's Early Learning Series, and a couple of books written by my dad to dovetail with my mum's system – *Tug the Pup* and *Max the Cat*. In the newsletter I attempted to convey to 'potential investors' the excitement of the opportunities; from shaving, to clothing, to education, and asked anyone who was interested in investing to contact me. As you might expect, the take-up was small: my mum and dad. To my delight, my mum offered to invest £2,000 of her pension into my venture when it was 'up and running'.

Creating momentum

As I sit here writing this, at my home in Marlow, it all seems like yesterday, not seventeen years ago. But, I guess when you've lived with it day after day, year after year, working out how to 'maximize the potential', then things stick with you. Looking back it all seems so terribly amateurish and badly thought out, but then all I was trying to do was to give one or two projects some momentum. Momentum, or as I like to think of it, rocking a boulder out of a hole that it has sat in for centuries, takes a long time. Backwards and forwards, side to side you rock it, so it gradually moves, faster and faster, until you break it free of the useless hollow it's been sitting in and hopefully to one side or the other of it is a hill, and it can start rolling downwards, gathering speed and energy. It's pointless rocking a boulder out of a hole that is at the bottom of a valley. This is where intelligence, timing and common sense come in. If I could rock the shaving-oil boulder from side to side and get it moving, then I could get another and another and another moving too. I worked on securing investment for Body Glove, I sent the first five chapters of my novel to a publisher, along with a synopsis for the trilogy and I spent a great deal of time trying to interest a publisher in Shirley's Early Learning Series.

One book that I read during this time was *Maverick!*, by a Brazilian businessman called Ricardo Semler. It's a fantastic, empowering and motivating read about how he inherited a Brazilian pump manufacturer, Semco, from his father and completely transformed it for the better, with the help and support of his employees. One of his ideas was to allow employees to set their own salaries, using their common sense. I did this at KMI for about six years. Another idea I recall was that you should take your watch off, put it in a draw and forget about time, the point being that whatever you were doing would only be slowed by you constantly checking on the time. This idea resonated with me, in fact, I took my watch off straight away and resolved to only wear it again when I felt KMI, King of Shaves was starting to look successful. It took five years.

Keeping the plates spinning

I didn't know it then, but I was in a classic 'plate-spinning' phase, i.e. trying to get a number of different projects up and running, with the hope that one of the 'plates' would spin with increasing speed and more stability, and that would be where my main focus would lie. That wasn't to happen for another three years, when it became clear that King of Shaves was going to be the brand that developed momentum, while Body Glove would be bedevilled by issues beyond our control and sadly fail.

Between January and September 1993 things happened very slowly and I got inexorably into more and more debt. This is where the 'E' in SPACE comes in. It is the key difference, in my opinion, between success and failure. 'E' stands for three words: enthuse, exceed and enjoy.

Enthusiasm is a trait you either do or don't have. I know many, many people who, if only they were enthusiastic about dealing with the challenges put in front of them, could be completely different. Other people can't make you enthusiastic, only you can be enthusiastic about solving tasks that seem insurmountable. It's a try, try and try again attitude. To exceed, i.e. be the best you can be, is also very important. The commercial world is highly competitive and there is no point setting up an average business. Just because you can create a product or provide a service is no guarantee anyone will bother buying it. For a business to truly work, it must:

1. Provide a product or service that no one else has
2. Provide a product or service that everyone will want
3. Price for profit
4. Price for sale

These four simple rules are known as the Harvard Rule of Four. They are so simple to remember yet these basic principles are often overlooked. In short, if you don't seek to exceed, you'll never succeed. The iPod is a brilliant example of a product that meets the Harvard Rule of Four.

The final 'E' is 'enjoy'. If you don't enjoy doing what you do, you can't expect anyone else to enjoy working with you. In the early days of any business when money is tight or non-existent, when no one knows who you are or what you do and you don't know whether or not you'll be a success or a failure, the enjoyment of what you do is paramount. To this day, I love doing what I do. I never thought I'd be out there 'changing the face of shaving for better, for ever' with King of Shaves, but I am and I love it. I know I won't do it for ever, I've given myself until 2012 to make King of Shaves a truly global brand, but if I *had* to do it for the rest of my life I'd love doing it. There is a huge freedom in running your own business, knowing what disaster looks like and comparing it with fantastic success, building a team you like around you and enjoying the challenges of a constantly changing commercial environment. Eeyores don't do enjoyment; Tiggers live for it.

So, between January and September 1993 I had to enthuse, exceed, enjoy, and that is what I did.

Chapter 7:
Enthuse,
Exceed and
Enjoy

Funding the dream

I had to secure funding for KMI. I reckoned I needed about £15,000 to get everything done – 10,000 bottles of shaving oil manufactured, brochures printed and money to cover overheads and expenses. As I said earlier, my mum offered to invest £2,000 of her retirement pension in the business, but I earned no money, I was living with my girlfriend whose mortgage I contributed to through unsecured loans that I'd one day have to pay off and I had the mortgage on my Streatham flat covered by rental income, with a small surplus. Fifteen thousand pounds seemed like an insurmountably huge amount of money to have to find.

One of the issues with the shaving oil was the small amount needed to achieve a great shave – two or three drops. This meant that only 10 millilitres or so of oil was needed to deliver 50–100 shaves. This was great for the consumer; the oil would last a long time, was easily portable, etc. and really quite good from a manufacturing perspective; buying the oil, filling a 10-millilitre container and packing it would be something that could, at a stretch, be done in a cottage-industry fashion (unlike filling cans with shaving gel, which would require a manufacturing line and specialist equipment). The big problem was the tiny oil bottle. How would it look on retailers' shelves next to a massive (200-millilitre) can of shaving foam or gel? I therefore designed a container that not only contained the shaving oil, but which could also spray water on to your face. As such it was a hybrid packaging solution that allowed the small amount of oil to be combined with a large amount of water, and the container looked bigger and better.

In researching and designing what the packaging solution might look like, I was alerted to the SMART award, which was sponsored by the Department of Trade and Industry (DTI), (now the Department of Business, Enterprise and Regulatory Reform). SMART stands for Small Firms Merit Award for Research and Technology. If you won the award, and could convince the DTI you had £15,000 of funding available, they would give you a further £45,000! Sixty thousand pounds of funding – that sounded worthwhile, so I applied for entry to the award and got into the first round.

I also decided to apply for a patent for my invention as it seemed the right thing to do. So for the first time I visited the Patent and Trademarks Office, then based in Southampton Row, London, to see what my chances of patenting my invention might be. I was hugely naïve. I had no idea you shouldn't show your invention to anyone prior to submitting it for a patent (this invalidates it) and to be honest, there was absolutely nothing patent-worthy about my container with oil at one end and water at the other! But it seemed the sort of thing Gillette would do, so I gave it a try.

As you can imagine, I didn't win the SMART award, but Herbie had been impressed with my efforts in applying for it and also the fact that I had secured a Training and Enterprise Council (TEC) grant of £50 every two weeks. The grant was dependent on me attending workshops, held in Ealing, which were really designed for local shopkeepers and small business owners, not for those with shaving brands with global aspirations. But, I attended these courses, gratefully took the government's money as investment in my business and used all my SPACE qualities to the full.

Sitting in a pub in Chesham, I asked Herbie if he might be

in a position to help financially with my shaving-oil business and provide all (or some) of the £15,000 I needed to get the business going. Herbie has always been very straightforward in my dealings with him. We'd known each other for a few years by now and he'd seen how hard I'd worked with Animal Republic, Body Glove and now with my shaving-oil idea, and that I had a passion and enthusiasm for it. Others might have seen a lack of focus and achievement so far as no one had made one pence of profit from any of my projects, but Herbie was good enough to say that if I found someone else to invest half the money, then he'd consider it.

You'll recall Pat Maris, one of my friends while at Portsmouth Polytechnic. He was working in the oil and gas-drilling industry by now and doing rather well, as indeed were many of my friends. He and I had remained close after I left poly. I invited him round for dinner and at the end of the evening I asked if he'd consider investing in KMI. I didn't tell him that I already had half of the funding in place, I just asked if he'd invest. He said, 'Yes, on the basis someone else invests in you.' So I explained that Herbie had agreed to put up £7,500 or so, and might he match it? He did.

However, when I came to register Knowledge Merchants International Ltd with Companies House, I was told I needed an international office to call it that. Having already, perhaps impetuously, had my letterhead printed 'KMI', I needed to come up with a new name. I liked the 'knowledge' so just needed a replacement word for 'international'. Knowledge & Merchandising Inc. Ltd was settled on, and on 13 April 1993, KMI was incorporated, company number 2808675, VAT number 627 0440 62 and with its registered address as my residence in South Ruislip.

The sun was rising on what was to become the UK's most

popular men's grooming brands! But there was a long, long, long way to go. After all, at this stage the brand 'King of Shaves' didn't even exist, and in fact in its first incarnation King of Shaves was called Sunrise (as men shave when the sun rises), its women's counterpart was to be called Sunset. (See page 101 for further explanation of the evolution of the brand name.) But I'm getting ahead of myself. Remember at this stage I've got a couple of businesses on the go!

Getting things done

The Body Glove business was starting to struggle. Sample clothing was now available for presentation to retailers, but time was ticking on and we'd missed the opportunity to present the range for the spring/summer season as the company in Holland hadn't been able to produce the stock. I had been able to secure investment in Body Glove from two other individuals who were consultant friends of Herbie's, one of whom, Tim McDowall, became a good friend of mine (sadly Tim died while on holiday in Mexico in 1995). Between them, the investors made available up to £50,000.

Despite my best efforts the house I shared with my girlfriend quickly took on the appearance of a warehouse, with boxes of clothing samples downstairs and all manner of shaving paraphernalia upstairs. Ann, my girlfriend, was generally supportive of what I was doing, as long as it didn't completely dominate our lives, which of course to a certain extent it did. For a couple of months in 1993 she decided not to renew her work contract and see what it would be like working alongside me.

The one capability you must have if you are to strike out on your own is to be able to motivate yourself to get things done.

For example, I wrote this part of the book while on a Virgin flight to Tokyo and I was lucky enough to be upgraded to Upper Class. The temptation was to sit back, enjoy a glass of wine and savour the surroundings. But, having taken off, my mind started to itch about getting stuff finished and my publisher wanted the manuscript for this book a month earlier than expected, so I needed to crack on with it. Business success comes with increasing momentum and the problem with momentum is that it can be lost easily by simply putting off doing what needs to be done.

Procrastination is your enemy and you must tackle it head on. The more you fill your day up with doing things, the more you'll find you are able to get done. The brain is a wonderful piece of kit and is able to deal with many tasks. 'Parallel processing' in the early stages of establishing a business – simply doing things sequentially – isn't good enough. In a way, you have to imagine yourself having already done the task and then work back from that point to where you are. Only then will you realize how much you have to do.

As I write this, I'm on a Shinkansen train (popularly known outside Japan as a bullet train) travelling between Tokyo and Gifu-Hashima, having spent the morning with our Japanese partner planning the launch of our Azor razor in Tokyo, visiting stores and trying to gain a better understanding of Japan. Back in 1993, my launch planning for the first King of Shaves shaving oil was a little less sophisticated, but it was important I launched the product correctly, nonetheless.

Getting into Harrods

My reasons for wanting to get the product into this store was that I needed to sell via a retailer that everyone knew and I needed volume. For some reason I had already decided that King of Shaves should be an international brand, and when looking at stores to stock it only one seemed to fit the bill – Harrods. From securing this one stockist I would then be able to approach a major chain, ideally Boots, and get them to list the product on the basis that Harrods were listing it. It seemed like a plan, so I tried to telephone the buyer at Harrods, only to be told that 'we don't give out buyers names' and 'you have to write, enclosing a sample of your product and presentation'. I didn't actually have a packaged sample of the product. I had a dummy bottle design and of course some sample oil which I'd blended from sweet almond oil and other essential oils.

This wasn't going to cut it. So I started my quest to physically manufacture the product. The first problem was who could make it? It may not sound like a difficult question now, with Google able to list suppliers of aromatherapy oils and details of potential manufacturing partners, but then it wasn't so easy. I'm sure there was a trade directory of manufacturers, but where to look? After all, making a shaving oil wasn't exactly something everyone was doing.

As often happens in times of challenge, a mix of fate and luck conspired to offer up a solution. And so it was later that week that I accompanied Herbie to Henley-on-Thames, where he was negotiating to buy a company called CCP, who specialized in market research on behalf of car dealers. I sat in the office (as part of his team!) and listened to the discussion, but it was a little boring, so after a short while I made my excuses and left to go wandering. Now, when I'm out and about my curiosity often takes over and I'll spend a lot of time taking in my surroundings, looking at the offerings in shops, seeing if anything unusual catches my eye. Having wandered into Henley, I came across a small chemist's that I thought I'd check out. Inside, I came across a shelf of essential oils branded Amphora Aromatics. I bought half a dozen of the oils and a bottle of carrier oil (essential oils are very powerful and have to be diluted with what's known as a carrier oil). There was also a book on aromatherapy, so I bought that too. When I got back home, I called directory enquiries and asked if they had a telephone number for Amphora Aromatics. Sure enough, they did, and I called them up, and asked if they might supply me with a blend of oils. I didn't tell them what for, fearing that if they knew you could shave with an oil, they might develop their own.

A few days later a parcel arrived from Amphora Aromatics containing some empty glass bottles and the oil that I had ordered. Meanwhile I'd been doing some experiments in the bathroom, mixing up a variety of essential oils, combined them with a new base oil (grapeseed) and through trial and error made a shaving oil that you only needed to use two or three drops of, as long as you kept your face wet throughout the shave.

It was clear that no retailer, let alone Harrods, would consider stocking the product without real packaging and some sort of brochure, so I called the owner of Amphora and said that I'd need enough oil to fill 5,000 or so bottles – just in case Boots were quick to place an order even though I'd yet to present to them. There was a silence at the end of the phone. 'I can't make that amount, Mr King. You have to understand, I sell dozens of bottles a week, not thousands!' Having actually driven in Ann's car to Amphora a couple of weeks previously, I was a bit annoyed that they hadn't told me then what they could and couldn't supply.

'So, what can I do?' I asked, not really in the mood to start the search for a shaving-oil partner all over again.

'Well,' he said, 'I could tell you who my supplier is . . .'

'Thanks,' I said, 'who is it?'

There was another pause. 'It will cost you,' came the reply.

I must say I was a bit taken aback. 'How much?' I asked.

'Two hundred and fifty,' he replied.

Once again my quest to shave the world was on. I put £250 on my credit card and as part of the negotiation he offered to tell me what quantities of essential oils would be needed for the carrier oil. Up until this point I had been using trial and error to get the right balance of oils in the mix. He said he would post me the details of his supplier, along with his thoughts on the trial formulation I'd come up with, as soon as my funds cleared. I gave him my Visa card number over the phone and true to his word, a couple of days later I had a nice handwritten note, a formulation for 'Kings Shave System' (see page 101 for further information on the brand name) and the key piece of knowledge – his supplier, a company based in Peterborough called Flavour Products International (FPI). Incidentally, Amphora Aromatics is now one of the UK's largest suppliers of essential oils!

Reading this now it all seems laughably amateurish. I don't know what Gillette would have thought about my product development process, but at the time it seemed the only way to get it done. While it lacked elegance, finesse and strategy, I had set out to obtain knowledge on manufacturing something that wasn't currently being made and when faced with barriers to getting it done, managed to get over or around them.

As I've alluded to already, this persistence, when combined with a passion to succeed, is a key quality found among pretty much all successful business founders or entrepreneurs. It is only you who can ensure something happens and if you are knocked back or held up it is only your desire to keep going that gets the job done. Sixteen years into building the King of Shaves brand, this passion and persistence still runs deep and strong within me. The challenges are sometimes a little larger or more complex than perhaps they were in the beginning, but all can be dealt with through working out how you can do it.

The evolution of a brand name

Lowestoft, Suffolk, is the most easterly point of the UK; this is where the sun shines first. On the basis that men shave in the morning, when the sun rises, I thought Sunrise would be a good name for the shaving oil. If I was to make one for women, then this could be called Sunset, as they might shave their legs prior to going out in the evening.

I guarantee you that had my shaving oil launched in its original guise, Sunrise, it would have sunk below the horizon almost straight away. Naming a product, and getting that name right, is critically important to brand recognition and customer retention. Brand naming is a multimillion-pound business, and as I had worked in advertising and marketing I knew I didn't have the funds to talk to a company like Interbrand (an international brand consultancy) about the name for my shaving oil.

So, for quite a few weeks the name Sunrise stuck with me, to the extent that I did some leaflets on PowerPoint, with a sun rising out of a blue ocean, and tried to write some copy about why shaving with Sunrise shaving oil would 'Change the face of shaving for better'. Hmmm.

It was about this time that my dad bought me a little book by John Guaspari called *I Know It When I See It*. It's well worth a read. It's about a fictional business called Punctuation, Inc., and how quality issues and lack of focus gradually cause it to lose business to a start-up called Process, Inc. Having read and reread the book, I looked at my Sunrise Shaving Oil and recognized that the performance was OK, but the look wasn't. I was enjoying my daily shave with Sunrise, but from a branding and design perspective, Sunrise wasn't really where it was at.

Given the title of the book I was reading, and my surname, it's perhaps obvious what the product should be called, but trust me, at that moment, it wasn't obvious to me at all. I flailed around for weeks until I came up with the concept of a 'shaving system'. This sounded quite technical and sophisticated and lent the product an air of performance, so I chose the name King's Shave System. (For the final evolution of the brand name to King of Shaves see page 116–117.)

By now I'd been able to convince a Leicester-based company called Measom Freer to let me have some prototype bottles, and had found a label manufacturer (remembered from my previous job) who could do a small run of labels. So, by July 1993 I had managed to design and manufacture a couple of dozen packs of Kings Shave System for Men and Sunrise Shave System for Women.

Despite repeated attempts to secure a meeting with Harrods, Boots and another potential retailer I'd identified – The Covent Garden General Trading Company – I'd managed to get nowhere. Letters I'd sent to potential development partners such as Creighton's, The Body Shop and M&S had been either ignored or I'd had a 'no thanks' reply. I was particularly annoyed with Creighton's, as following a telephone call they had agreed to meet me. I drove all the way to their head office in West Sussex, with my golden cardboard crown and presentation, only to be told they'd forgotten about the appointment and no one could meet with me.

Feeling frustrated, I decided to contact others retailers, specifically Selfridges and Bentalls (whose buying was handled out of their Kingston upon Thames store). Somehow or other, I was able to speak to an assistant at Selfridges, who said she'd see if the buyer was interested in meeting me. As I hung on the phone, my thoughts went back to Haymarket Publishing and selling ad-space for *Marketing* magazine: 'This could be the one; you never know; keep believing; she might meet me.'

And she did. The assistant buyer said if I could come along the following week, a lady called Sandra would see me. I was over the moon. Maybe if I got Selfridges on board first, then Harrods would realize what a great product it was and others would follow. Elated, I telephoned the buyer at Bentalls and had the second surprise of the day. She said she would meet me too, but not until October, as this was the first slot she had. 'Two in one day, I'm on my way,' I thought.

The next few days were spent pulling together my presentation for King's Shave System. I had the oil bottles packaged up and I made a professional-looking (well, in my opinion it was) counter-display tray to hold the bottles, twenty-five each of King's and Sunrise. After all, women would be shopping at Selfridges and maybe they'd buy Sunrise for themselves and King's for their partner.

'Is this it?'

Arriving early at Selfridges, I decided to look around the pharmacy department. I realized that what I was going to present would be very difficult for them to display, unless it was sited on the countertop, by the till – a prime selling location. The countertop had lots of Wilkinson Sword and Gillette Sensor razors on it (the latter had just launched), plenty of cans of shaving foam and the new-style shaving gel in a can.

I recall the buying department at Selfridges being a very compact space, full of desks, clothing hanging up and all manner of boxes and display items. It looked pretty disorganized to me, as I was ushered into Sandra's shoebox-size office. 'So, you're the guy who's going to revolutionize shaving are you?' were the first words I heard. Sitting opposite me, behind her desk, was an obviously no-nonsense sort of buyer, more used to dealing with fashion brands than a young guy peddling his shaving-oil wares. 'That's right,' I countered, 'I believe that King's Shave System will give men a chance to enjoy shaving, not endure it.'

'Hmmm. Let's see what you have then.' I proudly got out my box and leaflets. She looked at it disparagingly. 'Are these samples?'

'No, this is the counter-display unit,' I responded.

'You must be joking,' she retorted. 'People will think these are samples – they won't pay – how much? Two pounds ninety-nine for them! Is this it?'

'Yes,' I said. 'I know the packs are small, but you don't need much to get a great shave, and . . .'

'Well, if you don't need much, then what's the point of it?'

'If you have razor burn, like I do, it stops you . . .'

'We're not interested,' she said. 'This will never sell. I thought you had something worthwhile . . .'

Stung, and more than a bit upset, I apologized that the products obviously weren't suitable for her and backed out of the office. The meeting had not even lasted five minutes and all my hopes to get King's Shave System stocked by one of London's leading department stores were over.

Rather than go straight back home, I wandered aimlessly up

and down Oxford Street, thinking. What I'd presented had been, in my opinion, the best solution. But it was clearly a solution unacceptable to a commercial buyer. The oil bottles were viewed as worthless samples and too easily stolen. The price point at £2.99 was high, given the product had little external packaging or design to extol its value. There was little point in having men's and women's shaving oils alongside each other. As the buyer pointed out to me, they would have to be in different areas.

And the more I looked at what I'd spent hours designing and writing, let alone the money I'd spent printing my marketing material, the more I realized the product, in its current format, wasn't up to it. It was back to the drawing board. I had a meeting with Bentalls in October and between now (July) and then, I had time to get my act together. Oh, and I also had a surfwear brand to manage too!

Chapter 8:
Back to the
Drawing Board

Four mantras

In the preceding chapters I've attempted to put into words what skills I believe you need to get momentum going. I'm writing this chapter on my way back from a five-day business trip to Japan, to meet with the development and manufacturing team who have worked with us on our market-disrupting Azor razor, and to plan the launch for King of Shaves in Japan, in the Virgin Café in Tokyo.

Our host while in Japan, a senior manager of our partner company, was a guy called T.O. His role is key in translating our design and innovation requests to our manufacturing partner company. As we are 'zagging' while our competitors 'zig' (i.e. taking the unconventional path, rather than the safe, conventional one), this requires clear, concise explanation to make sure it is understood. The opportunities I see in developing King of Shaves to be a serious challenger brand to 'Wilkinette' (my nickname for Wilkinson Sword and Gillette) can easily be lost in translation, and T.O. is a master at explaining our often complex requests to his management team and senior directors.

Conversation with T.O. during dinner turned to the importance of simplicity in determining solutions for products and how hard it is to make something simple, yet supremely effective. T.O. explained that the fact I personally answered e-mails sent to me on a daily basis (at shave.com) was amazing, as was my use of the internet for blogging, news alerts, tweets and other cutting-edge stuff to keep on top of the business.

I explained that I had always done this, as I remembered a

slogan by the founder of the Japanese company Kyocera: 'Always retain a healthy degree of paranoia'; which to me meant keep close to the issues that affect your business and never be surprised by developments. Out of this discussion over dinner came four slogans or what T.O. would call 'Willisms'. They aren't necessarily original, and I'm sure others live by them, but they are worth spending a little time on before I come to getting the product listed in Harrods and spending two weeks hand-filling 10,000 bottles of shaving oil while standing at the kitchen sink. The four slogans are:

1. Consumer is cash
2. Same, but better
3. Change constantly
4. Different by design

Consumer is cash

When I put 'consumer' and 'cash' in the same sentence I'm not looking at the customer one-dimensionally in the form of a one-off sale. I'm looking at how we should see the customer, the individual who is singularly responsible for making any product or service a success or failure. You might expect me to say the consumer is king, i.e. he or she is always right, but that is not necessarily the case. Cash however is *always* right and every £4.99 that is spent on a King of Shaves Azor or AlphaGel is cash that is not being spent with one of our competitors.

To start up a business and continue to develop it successfully means you must constantly find out from the consumer if you are getting it right. This does not mean using a customer-care manager or a market-research firm to gauge opinion. This means *you*, the business manager, connecting with the consumer. Clearly, you cannot be with every consumer asking their opinion all of the time, but having a place to engage in dialogue with your customers is absolutely critical. I write two blogs. One is a King of Shaves-centric blog at shave.com/blogs/king and is 99 per cent to do with matters relating to King of Shaves and the parent company KMI.

The second blog is posted on brandroyalty.com and it is about everything that I think might interest people who want to understand what makes me tick, as well as King of Shaves. When I post on other people's blogs (if they are praising or criticizing our products) I always post as 'Will King, Founder, King of Shaves' and feel very close to the consumer through this one-to-one connection. When I'm in a Boots or Tesco store and see someone looking at the shaving products, I will politely introduce myself and often have a very interesting discussion about the brand, the company story or something else. This personal connection between brand owner (me) and consumer almost always translates into a sale or a dialogue that can be continued.

Making yourself accessible to those who are contributing to the growth of your business is absolutely critical, but this accessibility often wanes as a business grows older, bigger and more corporate. Where I'm concerned, I am healthily paranoid on a daily basis, whether we are exceeding our consumers' expectations or failing them. If only more CEOs were able to humanize their brand or service, then the messes companies get into by introducing unwanted products or services could be avoided. Although I'm a CEO, I'm a consumer too!

Same, but better

The 'same, but better' phrase is quite a neat one, and one that I'm delighted my competitors fail to exploit fully. To succeed in a market you need to constantly bring 'new' to the consumer. It's a cluttered world out there and 'new' can slice through clutter like a hot knife slices through butter. This is why car companies are always launching 'new' models for example (although they aren't actually that new at all, just the same old, same old, with the exception of the Smart, Prius and new Honda Hybrid).

However, always bringing 'new' to the market is a double-edged sword. Often 'new' involves 'more'; more cost, more features with dubious benefits, more packaging. So, I coined the phrase 'same, but better' when attempting to explain to our Japanese colleagues that we had no intention of moving our next generation Azor to six blades (or more), that in our opinion four was more than enough, three was adequate and if we could get back to a single blade that would be no bad thing! This is counter-intuitive, for in my market of multi-bladed, vibrating and trimming razors, all my competitors repeatedly launch 'new', which is always more expensive and not necessarily better. For example, Gillette's Fusion launch (the five-bladed razor) in 2005 has been nowhere near as mind-blowingly successful as their Mach3 (the three-bladed razor) launch in 1998. Why? Well, because adding two more blades, at a price nearly double that of Mach3 for replacement cartridges, didn't phenomenally improve the shaving experience. Adding a battery that allowed the razor to vibrate and apparently 'shave better' simply didn't, in my opinion, significantly enhance the product. After all, you don't drive a car around a racetrack that's vibrating all over the place do you? What it did allow the company to do was to bring 'new' to the market at an increased price, and give Duracell, who are owned by Gillette, a further channel to sell batteries. Energizer Holdings, the owner of Wilkinson Sword, followed suit. It's 'new' though involved adding a trimmer to an already large razor, again at a comparatively high retail price.

As we look to evolve the Azor razor, we have the twin mantras in mind of 'shaving simplicity' and 'same, but better'. I want our new cartridges to look largely like the old ones (because the old ones work well) but I want them to be better. When we improve our shaving software (our oils and gels) we aim to deliver to the consumer the same shaving experience, but better. This philosophy led to the introduction of the first Hybrid Shaving Oil (an oil emulsion), then the Hybrid Serum (an oil/gel emulsion, which is my shaving software product of choice). The serum is the original shaving oil, but better.

Change constantly

Embracing change as a constant is a behaviour I've practised for many years. If you're not evolving, you're dying in my view, and this goes for everything in a business. When change is unexpected then people, especially employees in a business, are very wary of it. But if your business is constantly changing, reinventing and challenging itself, this is very empowering. For example, where King of Shaves brands are concerned, the products are almost constantly changing in formulation (hopefully always being improved at no expense to the consumer). Our designs and brands are always being tweaked, whether through the introduction of new explanations (e.g. we came up with 'Prime, Shave, Protect' to explain the process of enjoying, rather than enduring your shave), new colours or entirely new products. Of course, some of the old products often have to go to facilitate the new, but if the product is the 'same, but better' then this is a good thing. As the founder of the business, if I am seen to be in favour of changing for the better then the team who work with me have the right not to do the same old, same old, day in day out, but to challenge the way they do things for the benefit of themselves and the business.

During the short life of King of Shaves I've seen a lot of companies and brands come and go, but there are a few that seem to be able to constantly reinvent themselves, just the way that Madonna does to keep her music fresh and her appeal as a celebrity. Apple, originally noted for products that enjoyed great design features and ease of use, manages to reinvent itself on a global level, by making things that are important to us easier – communication, leisure and enjoyment – with every new product they create. I'm writing this book on a three-year-old PowerBook, but it's quite heavy and in the last year or so Apple have brought out MacBook Air, which I was tempted to buy at the airport, but lugging two computers around with me didn't seem to make sense. There is nothing wrong with the computer I have; my nine-year-old son can make great use of it, but I have a desire to buy the next generation, for I genuinely believe it will be faster, lighter, better. With our Azor razor we are already introducing version two of the handle (we thought version one was about 90 per cent satisfactory) and are working on versions two and three of our cartridges. Some of our competitors have not changed their cartridges for the better for ten years; we are looking to change ours for the better just months into our launch!

Different by design

The shaving oil we launched typifies this phrase, as does the appearance, styling and packaging of our Azor razor. Failure to positively differentiate yourself in a competitive market will sound your death knell. Every day our lives are cluttered up with tens of thousands of distractions and disturbances; we enjoy only brief moments of quiet and reflection during the day. As these moments total a matter of minutes, the rest of your waking day is spent being distracted by a multitude of opportunities to move off the subject you're concentrating on, into a different space.

When I created the first King of Shaves shaving oil product it was genuinely different by design because to start with it wasn't a steel can of shaving foam. Because of this difference I was able to use the packaging to shout 'look at me – I'm different and better' and use this fact to gain valuable early publicity. If you're considering setting up a business, you must give clear thought to how you will differentiate your 'new' against the clutter of the 'old', which will try to asphyxiate you at every opportunity. This different by design approach is at the very core of pretty much everything King of Shaves does – whether in product, in publicity or in advertising. I have a simple take on it – is our product, service, ad, publicity, behaviour 'good, but different' (GBD)? If it isn't, then it's pointless doing it. If, however, it displays strong GBD credentials, then we get 100 per cent behind it. What King of Shaves has done is always bring GBD to the marketplace. This applies to our original shaving oil, our aloe-based AlphaGel and, of course, our Azor.

Starting again

Returning to my predicament following the disappointment of my meeting with Selfridges, I went back to Lowestoft to see Mum and Dad. The dogs, now eight months old, were still in their playful puppy stage and loved running along the beautiful sandy beach that Lowestoft is famous for, and I enjoyed some of Mum's Sunday roast and a chat with Dad about how KMI was coming along. Having designed the King's Shave System bottles and brochures, I'd taken some down to show him. While he thought they were 'nicely designed, but I'd expect that of you William' and the brochures 'well written' and that he enjoyed shaving with the oil (although we found out in the shower that the label ink that was supposed to be waterproof wasn't, when it all ran), he didn't think the name was particularly good. 'After all, what do you mean by Shave System?' he asked. I tried to explain. It was a different system of shaving, a better system, using an oil, that was all. In hindsight, it was a poor attempt to explain the product to the consumer.

As we were sitting in the kitchen, Dad asked if I wanted a quick game of cards before dinner. I'm not a fan of card games, so it was more to pass the time and temporarily distract me from thinking about my shaving oil that I played. A couple of hands in, he turned over the king of spades, and said spontaneously, 'Why don't you call it King of Shaves?' 'King of Shaves,' I thought, 'that's a bit steep, some people might take it the wrong way.' I said this to Dad. 'It's your name, isn't it?' he responded. 'I think it could work well. You could even have a king on a playing card and he's holding a razor instead of a sword, and he's shaved his beard off and is smiling! He'll have enjoyed the King of Shaves.' As we readied ourselves for dinner the cards were put away, but a seed had been sown that was to grow exponentially over the coming months.

'King of Shaves?' Herbie said, when I told him what I was going to call the shaving oil. 'I'm not sure about that. It's pretty long isn't it? It doesn't exactly say Nike or Adidas or Apple. I know you like it, but give it some thought.' Herbie and I are a good balance for each other, we are chalk and cheese in terms of what we're like, do and enjoy but there has been, and I'm sure, will always be, a healthy respect for each other's skills. While I was setting up KMI, he was running the Smile photo studio business, preparing for his own big day of opening. 'Well, I can't call it "Shave",' I thought to myself, thinking of his Smile business, and against my better judgement, settled for calling the first shaving oil 'King's' with the 'King of Shaves' slogan at the bottom of the pack.

I realized that the small 10-millilitre bottle of shaving oil would need to be attached to a larger card in order to display the product as something for sale, not something to be taken for free. Using PowerPoint, I designed the first packaging on the computer. Blue and black were the only two colours I could have (to make sure it was produced as cost-efficiently as possible) and the bottle would be held on a white card with a small plastic blister, which had yet to be made, let alone paid for. But hey, I had a product that worked for me. Every morning I would shout out 'Guess what I've just had?' and my girlfriend Ann would reply 'The King of Shaves'. Exactly. And soon, there wouldn't be just me enjoying the King of Shaves, there'd be tens, then thousands, then millions.

As a way of trying to keep money coming in during 1993, I'd been introduced via a friend to a couple of guys who'd raised some money to enter a yacht in the upcoming 1993–4 Whitbread Round The World Yacht Race (now the Volvo Ocean Race). The yacht was called *Dolphin* and was to be crewed by people with disabilities. It was a nice project; the guys behind it had managed to raise a couple of hundred thousand pounds, and I set about meeting companies and individuals on their behalf to try and secure additional sponsorship. The goal was to raise between £500,000 and £1 million.

The race started in September, and as it was July it was pretty clear that unless they got some money quick, the boat wouldn't be entering. However, they managed to get Reebok on-board as a sponsor, on the basis that the *Dolphin* campaign merged with another campaign, *Youth*, spearheaded by a young chap called Matt Humphries. To put it simply, the *Dolphin* project had a boat in build, but no money to campaign her; the Youth team had appeal to sponsors, but no boat. By merging, they had a complete campaign, *Dolphin and Youth*.

I was thanked for my involvement with helping the campaign, and invited down for the race start in the Solent. You'll recall from earlier in the book how much I loved Cowes and sailing, so this was a great opportunity to combine a bit of business with pleasure. When I first met Matt, who was the skipper and in charge of the combined project, I somewhat cheekily asked if King of Shaves could be their shaving sponsor if I supplied free product and five-figure sponsorship – £500.00. 'No problem,' he said. 'Good to have your support.' Although it sounds very little, £500 was a lot of money to me then. It was £500 I didn't have, and if I did it was almost certainly needed to pay for packaging or filling or bottling or postage or one of the many costs of starting up the business. But, I guess, every little helps, even on a big-budget, yacht-racing project, so prior to their departure I arranged to go down and get a photo of me with them. I had my first sponsorship deal, even though I had no retailer selling King of Shaves and no manufacurer on board. That *had* to change.

Taking the decision to move from 'potential' to 'reality' is a huge leap of faith. You have to have faith in yourself and others have to have faith in you. It's all well and good to have phrases like KISS, DIPADA and SPACE in your mind, to be zagging when others are zigging and to believe that 'one day I will be a challenger to Gillette'. But this physically has to happen. Product has to be made. Invoices need to be raised. Product has to be sold, and more importantly, bought again and again, otherwise your company is a one-off wonder and there are millions of those littering the wayside. I had two things I needed to do. I needed to get some actual printed bottles of King's, King of Shaves shaving oils made, get them filled by someone and get them packed into a cardboard box, ready for delivery. I was repeatedly trying to get meetings with Boots, I was still getting nowhere with Harrods and had my only confirmed meeting with Bentalls in October. I had to get real.

Registering the trademark

I realized that I needed some sort of protection and that I needed to think about trademarks. What if King's and/or King of Shaves was already trademarked or someone was using it? (We'll come on to my Australian problem shortly.) What about product insurance? Although I'd been quite happy shaving with the oil day in, day out, what if someone's face fell off when using it and sued me? Suddenly, lots of problems (and costs) started to come out of the woodwork. Where did you go to find out about trademarks? Who did you talk to about insuring your shaving oil? There was no one to do these things for me, so having concentrated on selling the product, I now needed to make it *and* make sure I could sell it.

Herbie told me that I should go to the Science Reference

Library in Southampton Row, London, to find out about trademarks. You could make an appointment to search trademark registers, and if your trademark wasn't already taken, file it for listing. So, off I went in search of a trademark. Little did I know that within a few years I'd be spending thousands of pounds with Marks & Clerk, leading trademark and patent attorneys, attempting to secure my legal right to call King of Shaves, King of Shaves!

Unlike now, when you can simply visit patent.gov.uk and perform an online search for trademarks (type in King of Shaves and you'll find us), then it was a book and microfiche-based system, where you had to sift through page after page of filing entries to see if you could list yours. It was quite a forbidding place, certainly not one I ever expected to find myself in. But needs must and as I didn't know about trademark attorneys (even if I did, I couldn't have afforded one), I started leafing through page after page of registrations in Class 3 (the toiletries classification).

After about an hour and a half I'd exhausted all the entries and been naturally delighted to see that no one had registered King's or King of Shaves. Just before leaving a thought propelled me to turn to the index and look for trademarks owned by certain companies, by Gillette in particular. Imagine my surprise when I discovered that Mr Gillette's first name was King! Gillette, founded by King Camp Gillette, was another King! 'Surely they must have trademarked King of Shaves,' I thought to myself, as I hurriedly raced through their entries of trademarks. Contour, GII, Sensor, but no King of Shaves. I can still feel my sense of relief that the king of shaving companies hadn't registered itself as the King of Shaves Company.

I asked the clerk how to apply for a trademark and was given a form to fill in and file with the trademarks office, which I hurriedly did, just in case someone from Gillette might file theirs. I remember being really scared that if I couldn't call my shaving oil King's or King of Shaves, then I'd have no business, would have wasted thousands of pounds and be no further on in changing the face of shaving for better, for ever.

Next on my list was to actually make some product.

Chapter 9:
Product is King

It's easy to make a product or get a product made, but building a brand out of a product requires that product to be truly great. If you have money, it's easy to make a shaving gel. You find a manufacturer of canned shaving gels, there are a couple in the UK for example, and you approach them to make you a product. The minimum quantity you'll probably have to order is 10,000, otherwise it doesn't make sense for the manufacturer to buy in the raw materials needed. Your problem is it won't be better (or worse) than any other shaving gel out there. This may not concern you; after all, you'll think, 'Gillette sell shaving gels, so can I.' Wrong. Why, after all, should anyone buy your shaving gel unless it is good, but different?

In the 1990s, L'Oréal, the massive French toiletries company, licensed the Harley Davidson (US motorcycle manufacturer) brand for a range of men's toiletries products. Did they sell? No. Why not? Well, what exactly was the relevance of a body spray or shaving gel with Harley Davidson on it? This is a prime example of doing something that might look obvious to the marketer (Harley Davidson is cool *ergo* a Harley Davidson body spray will be cool) but this is wrong.

With the shaving oil, I didn't have that problem. My shaving oil didn't look anything like what the competition were selling. It was a tiny 10-millilitre bottle, the competition sold huge 200-millilitre cans. Mine didn't foam up, theirs made you look like Santa Claus. You could travel lightly with my shaving oil, with a can you'd have to have a toilet bag.

'Different' was designed into the original King of Shaves shaving oil, in the same way we built difference into our Azor razor, launched in June 2008 (which will be explained in depth later in the book). Plus, the shaving oil was good (i.e. when I shaved with it I didn't suffer from razor burn or rash) whereas shaving with conventional shaving foam or gel I continued to suffer red, scratched skin. My marketing rationale was that 'If it works for me, then it will work for others.' QED.

I remember saying to Herbie, 'I've got a great brand here, H.'

He replied, 'Will, you've got a great product, one that works for you. It's not a brand, it may become one, but it's miles off a brand.'

I remembered this, and from simply looking at a product, constantly thought about how to evolve it into a brand.

As I mentioned earlier, Flavour Products International (FPI) were going to supply the shaving oil and Measom Freer Ltd the bottles. My initial meeting with the owner of Measom Freer Ltd, Mark Freer was enlightening. I pitched my King's for the King of Shaves shaving oil idea to him (at this time it was still in a small brown medicinal bottle with a dropper to dispense it) and he didn't lay waste to my ambitions. He was very straightforward and explained I'd need a standard 10-millilitre bottle made out of polypropylene, with a urethane cap and a plug with a hole in it so the oil wouldn't run out. He went away and returned with half a dozen of each of these elements. I looked at them – they were tiny – and asked if I could have a couple of hundred of each. I wouldn't say he rolled his eyes, but he sort of stared at me and explained that there was a 'MOQ'.

'What's that?' I asked.

'Minimum order quantity,' he replied, 'and we'll have to have payment pro forma.'

In advance in other words.

'Oh. What's the MOQ amount?'

'Ten thousand' was the reply.

Ten thousand! I was hoping my first order would come from Harrods or Bentalls, but they were only two outlets, and even I knew they'd only be selling a few dozen a week, if that. Ten thousand bottles. I was continuing to be passionately persistent with Boots, and convinced myself that if they ordered, of course I'd need 10,000. Mark said, 'If you can order ten thousand, we can supply them within a couple of weeks. As long as you can prepay, we can think about setting you up as a supplier.'

I returned back home thinking, 'If this is what it's going to be like with a standard bottle, what about the display card, the plastic "blister" that I'll need to hold the bottle on the card and the cardboard box to package the bottles in?' It's important for me to say at this stage I simply had no understanding of these issues. Clearly, someone coming from a background in product manufacture would, and maybe it looks like I was a bit naïve, but, as I had no idea of the challenges of manufacturing the shaving oil, hurdles that were put in my way simply had to be overcome. I didn't dwell on them, I just thought to myself, 'Oh well, best work out how I can buy all of this stuff and get it sold.' In many ways, it refocused me on the volume side of the business, as no one was ever going to challenge 'the best a man can get' with a few dozen sales out of Harrods.

I got hold of Herbie and explained I'd need to find some money to pay Measom Freer, and that I had also identified potential manufacturers for the backing card, the printing of the card, the plastic 'blister' that would be stuck on the backing card to hold the bottle and a company who could warehouse the stock – a Slough-based company called Packaging Supplies. He asked, 'How much?'

I said, 'I think, about five thousand pounds.'

There was a short silence on the line, then, 'OK, when do you need it by?'

I didn't know, so I said, 'In the next couple of weeks or so.'

At the start of this book, I explained that it is rare that one individual can do it all, from start to finish, without recourse to someone who is prepared to share the risk alongside you, but with a different perspective. Although I enjoyed the support of my girlfriend, she was no longer directly involved in the business, and certainly didn't have access to £5,000. My parents had invested £2,000 and I didn't want to keep asking them for money. At the time, one of my brothers was working in the US, starting off his career, and unavailable, and my other brother, a successful grain-trading manager, thought I should 'go back to doing what I was good at doing' and at that time wasn't up for investment (he's a major investor now!). So, Herbie was pretty much my lifeline and from somewhere (his wife Suann's savings accounts) was able to get me a few thousand pounds to keep King of Shaves going.

One down, only 9,999 to go!

At this point, I must make it clear that I couldn't have got King of Shaves going without Herbie's invaluable and hugely appreciated support. He was backing my belief that I could somehow make a product, get it stocked, do some marketing to make people aware of it and sell some on a profitable basis. He certainly wasn't backing the product as a 'killer application'. He didn't have issues shaving himself, but I think he saw in me a drive and determination to bring my shaving solution to a wider market. I've no doubt that if he hadn't been able to come up with the money, I'd have found some from somewhere, probably taking on more credit-card debt (which I had a lot of already) or by asking Mum and Dad again. But, it was a business, I believed in the product, I believed the business would be a great business and as he was my business partner I felt that Herbie would help. And he did.

I was left with one final problem; actually getting the oil mix into the bottle. This is called contract filling and in many cases can be handled these days on a full-service basis. By which I mean there are contract manufacturers who buy all the components, make the product and then sell the finished item to the purchaser, i.e. me. But at this point in time no one had made a shaving oil in the UK, I didn't know of any such manufacturing companies and I'd already bought the components. I made enquiries with various companies about filling the bottles but they didn't really want to know. Either their line wasn't set up to fill this tiny bottle or they insisted on buying in the raw materials themselves (no doubt at a slightly inflated cost to me) or there was some other issue.

So, in July 1993 there I was with a garage containing two massive cardboard boxes, each holding 5,000 bottles, a box containing 10,000 plugs, another box containing 10,000 white urea caps and 100 litres of blue-coloured shaving oil in two 50-litre plastic drums. Luckily, I had found out from a discussion with the printer that the bottles had to be printed first, before they were filled. If they were filled first and then sent for printing, it would be likely that some of the oil would leak out and would contaminate the plastic. Imagine if I hadn't known that, and had had the bottles filled then sent for printing, I'd have had to write off the entire run! But fortune smiled on me. So, having designed the logo for the first ever King of Shaves oil (a crown, how original) and laid out the words 'King's' with 'King of Shaves' underneath, I sent the bottles off for printing. 'How long?' I asked.

'A month,' was the reply.

'You're joking,' I exclaimed, 'I need to get them filled, packed and ready for [i.e. in anticipation of] my first order.'

'It's factory shutdown in August, you'll be lucky to get them in a month. Do you want us to print them or not? If you do, we'll need payment in advance.'

Having no other option, I agreed.

My first sales

I'd designed the display backing card on my computer, using just two colours (to keep costs down) and Ann had got it printed at her work. The business was still based in the small upstairs bedroom. I was surrounded by stuff and I had filled about a hundred bottles of oil myself. At this stage, the only person who'd really used the shaving oil was me. Ann mentioned that during the lunch hour at her work, small business vendors could come in and sell their product (normally greeting cards and the like). I thought this sounded like a good opportunity to sell some bottles of shaving oil and get some customer feedback, so she arranged for me to have a little stall and sell the oil. I sold about ten bottles at £2.99 each, along with supplying an instruction leaflet explaining razor rash and razor burn. I think most of the purchasers took pity on me, Ann had sent down quite a few people from her office to buy my shaving oil. It was clear then, however, that the concept of shaving with oil needed quite a lot of explanation and unless the man actually had a problem shaving then he didn't really see the need for it. In some ways I was quite deflated by this, as I'd assumed that a lot of men suffered from razor burn and rash, when quite clearly they didn't. But I still enjoyed the King of Shaves every morning and put these niggling worries to the back of my mind.

In mid-August 1993 the 10,000 printed bottles were returned, in the same cardboard boxes as I'd sent them away in, nicely printed and needing to be filled. I'd been unable to find a contract manufacturer and on opening the garage door the two containers of blue oil stared back at me. I closed the door, thinking, 'I'll find a way around this.'

Alongside the KMI business, I was also dealing with the start-up phase of the Body Glove clothing distribution. This business, in its entirety, was also being run out of my home, with boxes of sample T-shirts and sweatshirts being stored in the garage, alongside the boxes of components for King of Shaves. We'd also been introduced to a company that had licensed the Body Glove brand on to a range of sunscreens called Skin Patrol, which were made in the US, and were available for sale alongside the clothing. In for a penny, in for a pound, we agreed to become the distributor for the sunscreen products too.

I guess you sense the situation at that time; a lot of plates being spun simultaneously, a lot of detail that needed dealing with and a lot of belief. In hindsight, there was far too much going on; a surfwear brand here, a sunscreen range there, a shaving product and, amazingly, at the same time my mum and dad were still keen on developing the Shirley's Early Learning Series range of books. We had a very loose discussion about the books with an educational publisher, but this seemed to be going nowhere.

I had a ton on, too much, in fact. But somehow or other my brain seemed able to cope with the myriad tasks that needed to be done. I felt 'the more I have on, the better', as I thought that at least if one plate stopped spinning, others would keep going. I knew I was capable of handling the pressure and even if I wasn't I'd never let anyone else know, as they were investing their hard-earned cash in me and my ideas to bring them to successful fruition.

Over the summer I'd been repeatedly calling the toiletries buyer at Harrods to try and get a meeting to show her my product. Having sent some early product through for her to review, she'd come back and said that she had some interest 'but Harrods can't sell the same product as other retailers'.

'What?'

'Well, we don't want to sell the same as other stores,' she explained. 'Maybe you can do an exclusive for us?'

Can you imagine? Still no guarantee of an order and no retailer wanted what I was producing. But, I got back to Measom Freer, asked what other bottles they had and settled on a 25-millilitre bottle of oil that I thought I could sell at £5.99 in Harrods on an exclusive basis. Mark, to his credit, allowed me to buy just 1,000 of these (and I was able to pay after thirty days). These needed to be printed too, and as I needed to have the Harrods exclusive product to show the buyer, they went off for printing. I also found a packaging solution that would work with this bigger bottle that didn't require tooling for (another) plastic blister.

As my job prior to being made redundant had been in the area of corporate events and entertaining, I thought the forthcoming Whitbread race in September would be a great opportunity to invite some buyers along to an event. I had a lot of friends in sailing and through a couple of contacts was able to borrow two yachts for the day. I'd be on one, with one of my sailing friends, Kim, on the other. Why two yachts? Well, I guess I thought potential buyers would be impressed with that, after all, two yachts are better than one!

Through a sail-making friend I had a couple of battle banners (large flags) manufactured from offcuts of sailing cloth. One read 'King's, King of Shaves', the other 'Sunrise, The Perfect Shave' – my shaving oil for women. These cost about £500 and when they arrived I was super-excited, until I found out they'd been made from really hard sailcloth, which meant they made a huge racket in a wind.

In the week prior to the race starting, I travelled down to the newly completed Ocean Village marina in Southampton, where all the yachts were moored, and did a photoshoot with Matt Humphries and his crew of *Dolphin and Youth*, with me ceremoniously handing over my cheque, with the King of Shaves flag draped over their main boom.

Again, looking back, it all seems incredibly naïve and amateurish, but it was genuine, honest, exciting stuff. I had arranged it all, I'd made it all happen and we were an official sponsor of a round-the-world racing yacht. The race started and I was joined on my yacht by my dad Tony, Herbie and a friend, Jeremy Warren, who took some great photos from being hoisted up the mast. As we motored out towards Spitbank Fort off Portsmouth, where the race was due to come through, my dad played his accordion (he'd recently learned) with a ditty that went:

King of Shaves, King of Shaves,
Over the waves, with the King of Shaves,
Sunrise too, good for you,
We all shave together.

I still have the piece of paper with the lyrics on it.

The only buyer we'd been able to convince to come along worked for the (now defunct) Covent Garden General Store.

She brought her young son and we all had a fantastic time watching these fast-racing yachts smoke past us, spinnakers up, en route around the world. 'One day, I'll have my own yacht,' I said to myself, 'one day.'

Chapter 10: Don't Stop, 'Til You've Put on 10,000 Tops

Ten thousand bottles sitting in the box,
Ten thousand bottles sitting in the box,
And if one little bottle should be filled right to the top,
There'll be nine thousand nine hundred and ninety-nine
bottles, sitting in the box . . .

Of all the things about the start of King of Shaves, the verse above perhaps signifies most the attitude you have to take to get things done. Looking again at my SPACE acronym, it was now time to combine the attitude of action with passion and persistence and get two things achieved. First, the manufacture of the product and second, a retailer to bring the King of Shaves to the public.

It was becoming clear to me that filling the bottles was a real problem. I didn't have any money, I didn't want to ask any of the investors for more money and I'd been unable to find a company to fill the newly printed bottles for me. So, that left me. I brought a few bottles into the kitchen and wondered how I could fill them without spilling any oil. A funnel proved no use at all as it was impossible to accurately measure the amount and it was incredibly messy. I took the dogs out for their lunchtime walk and thought about how to solve my problem. I then remembered that a friend of mine, Keith Jackson, worked at an Isle of Wight-based company called SP Systems, which specialized in the manufacture of advanced composites (carbon fibre and the like). I knew that the resin had to be accurately dosed into the sheets of fibre to make them stiff and hard. I called him up, and said, 'Keith, I need to get ten millilitres of liquid into a small bottle without wastage or mess. Any ideas?'

'Willie, you need a gunk pump,' he said.

'A what?'

'A gunk pump, it's a pump that can accurately dispense small amounts of resin. I'll see what we have and if I can find one for you I'll post it to you, OK?'

True to his word, a few days later I took delivery of a white Englass pump, with a note from Keith saying that it would accurately dispense 2 millilitres per pump. 'Good luck,' the note ended.

I manhandled one of the 50-litre plastic drums from the garage into the kitchen and set it up on the kitchen worksurface. Even as I write this, sixteen years on, I can feel my heart race. Would it work? I managed to cut a hole in the cap and screwed the pump either side of it. I started pumping, then realized I'd need an oil bottle, so grabbed one, only to find that the width of the pump dispenser was too wide to fit inside the neck of the bottle. I looked around for a knife and pared down the pump dispenser to make sure it would fit snugly. Then I pumped. Lo and behold, once the pump had been primed, every pump dispensed 2 millilitres. The first few were a bit messy, as I was getting used to the rhythm, but within ten minutes or so I'd mastered it.

Hold bottle in left hand
Push bottle under pump dispenser
Pump one (2 millilitres)
Pump two (4 millilitres)
Pump three (6 millilitres)
Pump four (8 millilitres)
Pump five (10 millilitres)

Check bottle is OK
Push in plug
Twist on cap
Put into cardboard box

So, I'd started. I didn't think 'I'll start this tomorrow' and take myself off and do something else, maybe call another buyer or dream up another advertising campaign for King of Shaves. No, I simply got on with it. I remember starting at around 2.30 p.m. and later that evening was still pumping when my girlfriend arrived home. 'I've done about three hundred,' I said, trying to distract her from looking at her nice kitchen that was now littered with boxes, gunk pumps and gloop. 'Well done, I'll give you a hand after dinner.' I'm sure she wanted to say quite a few other things, but now I had my very own bottle of shaving oil to shave with and only had a further 9,700 to fill.

Over the next ten days, after dropping Ann at the Tube station, I'd settle down and carry out the same routine of filling the bottles, only stopping at lunchtime to walk the dogs. I got a massive blister on the palm of my right hand, which was very painful and meant I had to take things slower. I got calluses on my fingers too, from pushing in the plug and twisting on the top, but I just got on with it, and in a funny way, almost looked forward to the task each day. As each cardboard box filled up with bottles it felt that my product was getting closer and closer to reality, and after a fortnight (I didn't do it at weekends, that would have probably killed my relationship stone dead) I looked back with a lot of pride on my 10,000 filled bottles.

As well as filling the 10-millilitre bottles, I also had enough oil to fill up 500 of the 25-millilitre bottles, which was a little more awkward as this required more pumps and guesswork as to the final few millilitres.

The lesson I took from this was the importance of persistence and just getting on with it. So many people I've met in my life have said to me, 'If only I'd done what you've done, I could be successful too!' and I'd say, 'Well, you can do it, what's stopping you?' What would follow would be reason after reason about not having the right idea or some other excuse. I knew it had to be done, I was relentless about getting it done, a sense of pride took over and when I'd finished, I knew I'd done something no one else was willing to do, and I'd saved my fledgling company about £2,000, money I didn't have.

Harrods' switchboard number is engraved on my mind forever – 071 730 1234 (or 0207 730 1234 as it is now). It's one I called regularly to try and speak with the men's grooming and toiletries buyer. I finally managed to speak with her in late August, and she agreed to give me ten minutes of her time during September, requesting that I sent in some samples of the oil, pricing and anything else that would be useful for her in making a decision. I duly pulled this together, and explained that the packs were a mock-up, as the real ones were currently being printed. I looked forward to explaining to her how King's, King of Shaves would make an ideal addition to Harrods' shelves.

The prospective meeting never transpired, so week after week I'd call and ask if I could meet with her or if a decision had been made. I'd repeatedly get her assistant, who'd say: 'It's on her desk, she'll be looking at it shortly' or 'Yes, she's looked at it and is going to get back to you soon' or 'She's out at the moment, but I know she's talking to someone later.' This went on for weeks and I was getting despondent. I had a meeting coming up with Bentalls in October and was desperate to be able to tell them, 'Harrods are listing the twenty-five-millilitre pack at five pounds ninety-nine. I'd love Bentalls to list King's too.'

Herbie asked how I was getting on, as he was approaching the launch of his Smile studio, and I always said 'I'm nearly there, I'm just waiting to hear back from Harrods.' One day, I went down to the photo studio in London where he was overseeing the photography of models to be used in the studio and the photographer kindly snapped a few rolls of me holding a bottle of the shaving oil.

Still no news from Harrods.

Taking a gamble

It was then I decided to take a gamble. I justified it to myself by saying that unless I broke the impasse I seemed to be in with Harrods and got the product listed, all the money that friends and family had invested in me would be wasted. I thought about the £2,000 my parents had invested; the thousands of pounds that Herbie had managed to find; the fact that Pat Maris, my best friend from poly, had backed me and that I'd spent nearly a year making an oil to shave with. It was time to up the ante.

Mr Al Fayed's private office please. It's Mr King calling, he's expecting my call.

Good afternoon, this is Mr Al Fayed's personal assistant, how may I help you?

Good afternoon, my name is William King and I'm the owner of King's King of Shaves shaving brand. I've been unable to find out from your toiletries buying office whether or not Harrods are stocking King of Shaves. I very much want Harrods to be my first stockist and I am starting to get enquiries for the product. Please might I fax Mr Al Fayed a copy of the letter that your buyer has? As I would hate for Harrods to not be the first stockist of King of Shaves.

Pause.

Certainly, Mr King. Here is my private fax number. Mr Al Fayed is out at the moment, but I'll be sure to show it to him when he returns.

I pulled out the latest copy of my fax to the buyer and faxed it to Mr Al Fayed's personal assistant with a covering note. And waited.

I explained to Ann what I'd done when she arrived back later that evening, and she just said, 'Will, you did what you felt you had to do.' Looking back on it now it was a huge gamble, one I've never replicated since, because it could have gone one of many ways. Mr Al Fayed's PA could easily have forwarded my letter to the buyer with a note reading 'Please deal with this', the buyer would have seen I'd tried to go over her head and probably told me I'd never supply Harrods. Or, his PA could have simply shredded my fax and when I called back explained that 'Mr Al Fayed says there is nothing he can do. Harrods are not interested in your product.'

But when I awoke the next morning and went into the small bedroom that served as my office and glanced at the fax, there was a fax from Harrods, along with a purchase order for twenty-five bottles of King's King of Shaves shaving oil at £2.12 each, plus VAT. I'm trying to put what I felt into words, but can't. It was my first order. It was real. It existed. It was from Harrods. The world's best shave was stocked by Harrods, the world's best-known department store.

I was elated. Later that morning, I called Harrods buying department, to thank them for buying King of Shaves.

Is Miss P there please?
No.
Oh, please can you tell her 'thanks for the order'. I know King's will sell really well out of Harrods.
Silence.
She's moved to another department. Goodbye.

Years later, I came across the buyer, who was by now a senior buyer at a leading London department store.

You really wanted Harrods to stock King of Shaves.
Yes, I did. It was the difference between success and failure for me, my business and my investors.
I know. You're doing really well.
Thanks! No hard feelings . . .
No hard feelings Will, you did what you felt you had to do.

Filling the 10,000 bottles and getting Mohamed Al Fayed to personally list King of Shaves in Harrods in 1993 were defining moments for me, followed by Bentalls also listing the product following my meeting with them. I had a long way to go, but I had the most famous store in the world stocking my product and I was on top of the world. At least for now.

It's hard to remember now the many other things I had to sort out when launching the oil. Product liability insurance was provided by Michael Aston of London-based insurance broker Ashley Milton. Michael asked how much I thought I'd be selling in the first year. 'About three hundred pounds, I think.' After he'd finished laughing, he asked me to fax over what was in the product and who the manufacturer was. He gave me a quote of about £500 or so, I think, for £2 million product liability cover. I'd found out all about barcodes and designed myself a programme that allowed me to make one. The very first barcode was 5 026442 18866 8. Funny the things you remember.

Shaving and surfing

In the last six months I've had two evenings celebrating the satisfaction of success. In November 2008, King of Shaves won the Confederation of British Industry (CBI) and *Real Business* magazine's Growing Business Award, with the ceremony being held at the Marriott Grosvenor Square, London. Recently, we were back at the same location for the *Growing Business* magazine's Fast Growth Business Awards ceremony, where we won not one, but two awards: Best Product Company and the overall Fast Growth Business Award. Herbie and I were delighted. Having set up KMI, King of Shaves nearly sixteen years ago, it just goes to show that you really have to have a persistence to succeed, and that when success starts showing its face, then you can get the business into a strong cycle of continuing growth and further success.

But back in autumn/winter 1993, winning awards were the very furthest thing from my mind. We'd supplied the first order of 25-millilitre bottles to both Harrods and Bentalls, and each was selling between six and twelve a week. Not exactly a stellar sales number, but from just me shaving with King of Shaves, now we had (hopefully) a few dozen converts.

The blister for the 10-millilitre pack had been produced and in November I was expecting to take delivery of 5,000 of each of the King's, King of Shaves and Sunrise The Perfect Shave products, all boxed and ready to be sold. I had no idea where they'd be stored though!

I did some photography of the product in the garden when the sun had been shining, and in the bathroom, and created a press release that I sent out to a few magazines. The first ever piece of press coverage we secured was in *Boards* magazine, a windsurfing monthly that I read. I thought the natural feel of the shaving oil might appeal to surfers and windsurfers. The product got a nice little write-up and photo. I had my first piece of genuine publicity.

As well as trying to secure press coverage, albeit in a somewhat amateurish fashion, I packaged up my very first 25-millilitre bottle of King's and sent it first class to Prince Charles, with a brief covering letter. He didn't write back personally, but one of his staff did, saying that the prince had been 'delighted' to receive the first ever King of Shaves product and that he wished me 'every success' with the business. I'd met Prince Charles some years back, when Hedges Wright, the conference production company I'd worked for, produced the Prince's Trust tenth-anniversary birthday party, which was held at the Limelight (now the Outback) club in central London. I'd not been introduced to His Royal Highness personally, but was glad I'd been able to work with the Prince's Trust.

I remember that as 1993 drew to a close my shaving oil was on sale and against all the odds seemed to be selling. This was, of course, a huge relief. I had two stockists, but I needed to nail Boots. The buyer there was a lady called Fiona Kemp. She must have got so fed up hearing my voice requesting a meeting or getting another letter or fax explaining why I believed King's would sell well in Boots, that I'm sure she finally just gave in to get some peace. 'Will, I can't see you before Christmas, but let's put a date in the diary towards the end of January, early

February. We don't have a range review until May, so this is the earliest we can meet you.'

February! It was late October! What was I going to do until February? I didn't want to approach other retailers like Sainsbury's, then the biggest UK supermarket chain, or Tesco, as I'd looked at their shaving fixtures and it seemed to be wholly dominated by Gillette and Wilkinson Sword. Boots seemed to offer a safer, more relevant haven for King of Shaves, but I couldn't meet the buyer until February. Aaargggh!

As there was very little I could do to accelerate KMI's business, I turned my attention to the company that would become Core Brands Ltd, the Body Glove UK fashion distributor. The other investors had provided the cash to buy two sample collections of clothes (as required under the as-yet-unsigned distribution contract) and in early November four massive cardboard boxes arrived at the house. More clutter! Ann and I eagerly tore the boxes open and went through the dozens of samples. The designs were eclectic to say the least. Remember, Body Glove is a Californian wetsuit and surfwear brand, but because a Dutch company had the master licence they'd designed their own take on it, with garments ranging from leather jackets to bright orange (the Dutch love their orange) T-shirts and board shorts.

It wasn't love at first sight. But, what to do? Looking back now, we should have learned a lesson very quickly: if you're not in control of the product, you're not in control of the business. We had little or no say over the design direction. Don't get me wrong, the clothes were well made and even today my dad has a Body Glove coat and T-shirt that he wears, sixteen years on. But fashionable? No.

However, the brand name was becoming increasingly well known and many people when they looked at KMI and Core

Brands, believed Body Glove would be 'huge' and as for King's, 'well, I'm not sure . . .'

Combining pleasure with business

I'd been working pretty much twenty-four seven since the start of the year and to be honest was pretty wiped out. My girlfriend offered to take me on an early-season week's skiing in Val d'Isère, with a company called Bladon Lines, then well known for offering affordable, yet good-quality skiing holidays. So, in early December we left the UK for Val d'Isère, having no idea whether there was any snow there or not until we arrived in the beautiful resort. There was snow aplenty and I was really looking forward to a week of rest and recuperation.

The bartender in the chalet we were staying in was quite a cool young chap by the name of Ivan, he played the guitar and was good value entertainment. 'Want to rent a snowboard?' Ivan casually asked one evening while I was in the bar having a drink. 'A mate of mine, Andy Hill, rents them. He lives in Tignes but is willing to drive up tomorrow and fit you out.'

'Sounds good,' I answered. 'Is it hard?'

Ivan laughed, 'I'm sure you'll pick it up, Will.'

Little did I know he was setting up a meeting with a guy who was to join me as one of our first employees, and who is still with me sixteen years later, now in his early forties!

Andy arrived at the chalet the following evening, a wiry, enthusiastic guy with a Vision snowboard that looked brand new. I was impressed. 'It's eighty francs for the day. I'll give you a couple of tips. I'm sure you can work the rest out,' Andy said.

'How hard can it be?' I thought to myself. I was good at skateboarding and windsurfing, this looked like windsurfing on snow.

Afterwards, we had a drink and a brief chat. It turned out he worked as a builder in the UK in the summer, earning enough to allow him to pursue a semi-professional snowboard career in the winter. He was a member of the British snowboard team and had a couple of small sponsorship deals. 'What do you do?' he asked.

'Well, I was in marketing but I was made redundant and I've just launched a shaving oil and alongside that have set up a company to distribute Body Glove clothing. Do you know it?'

Indeed he did, and although we didn't really talk a great deal further, he seemed like a nice, genuine, hard-working chap, out there doing what he loved in the winter, paying for it by working in the summer.

Andy recalls:

I first met Will in 1993 when he was one of my punters and little did I know then that I was to spend the next thirteen years working for and with him! In 1993 I was running a snowboard-hire business with a mate to support our life as pro-snowboarders in Val d'Isère.

I've always believed in good customer service, so we took our snowboards to the punters, rather than them needing to come to us. We couldn't afford the overhead of a shop. Will was in his late twenties back then, with curly blond hair, plenty of nervous enthusiasm, passion and belief. Even back then Will didn't really do small talk, he did business talk and it was in a conversation in the bar after his day snowboarding that he told me about his latest ventures, one being a shaving oil and the other a surf and snowboard clothing range called Body Glove that he was importing into the UK. At the time it was the latter that caught my attention as we were always looking for potential sponsorship. Hence his name and address went into my little black book for future reference.

We returned from a nice break to a cold UK, two dogs who'd missed us and a house full of boxes. And I'd met a future employee. What a year.

Returning to SPACE and the satisfaction of success, it's vitally important that you don't just work, work, work and never relax. Of course, you *have* to work hard, but you should also try and plan timeouts that allow you to recharge. Every week, one of my little treats was going to a curry house in Ruislip, enjoying a cold beer, a hot curry and a chat. It was a break from the grind of seeming to go nowhere on a daily basis, having a dream about the future and a little respite from the day's challenges.

I hadn't expected to become a founder of not just one, but two businesses. As you're reading this, you may not expect to be made redundant or have the chance or opportunity to do something different. I'm just like you. Something happened to my way of life, I had to adapt to that change and shape it to my advantage. No one did that for me. It was my decision to do it and that decision was born out of an anger and frustration at my life being messed up by other people and a belief that I could trust myself to be successful.

Helping Herbie launch his business

One notable event before 1993 drew to a close was getting Mr Blobby to open Herbie's Smile studio in Watford. A PR friend of mine, Brian MacLaurin, looked after Noel Edmonds and *Noel's House Party* was a huge Saturday TV draw. I knew Herbie wanted something special to launch Smile and who better than Mr Blobby! Brian had been masterminding the release of Mr Blobby's Christmas single (which actually went to number one) and Mr Blobby was very high profile. For about £600, we managed to do a deal whereby Mr Blobby would be smuggled into the Harlequin Centre, run around and generally terrorize people, which he did to great effect. Kids screamed, adults laughed and Mr Blobby ran amok, drawing really big crowds.

The importance of publicity and leveraging what you've got to a wide audience was rammed home to me at this point. While I'd worked in the corporate communications industry I'd got to know Brian MacLaurin, who was in the process of setting up MacLaurin Communications, a hugely successful PR company that he sold in 2001. Although I was pretty young and naïve, he took a shine to me and we often talked about the 'black art of media management' and how critical it was to a company's success.

KMI moves on

If 1993 was a year of hectic start-up, 1994 was the same but ten times as hard. It was also the year that KMI started to grow in a meaningful way and I probably learned the most in one single year that I'd ever learn. It was time to grow.

In early 1994 it was clear to me that my attempts at product PR weren't exactly hitting the mark, and although I'd secured a couple of pieces, we were way off getting into major style magazines and newspapers. I sat down with Brian MacLaurin, then in small offices in Victoria with just a couple of staff, and asked him, 'Will you do my PR for King's?'

'Sure,' he said, 'I'll get you a proposal. When do you want it to start?'

'Well, I hope to be in Boots in April/May, so maybe around that time?'

'OK, Will. As you know, many magazines work three months ahead but let's see what we can pull together.'

'How much will it cost me?'

'About ten thousand pounds.'

'Ten thousand pounds! For how long?'

'Six months should do it.'

Jeez. I had to find more money, but put that to the back of my mind. I hadn't had the proposal yet and I wasn't going to tell Brian I had no way of paying him. I'd sort something out.

Ann and I had taken the decision to move out of South Ruislip, to rent her house out and find somewhere in the country. Herbie lived in Chesham, a small town in Buckinghamshire, and we'd looked at houses to rent in Beaconsfield and in Chalfont St Giles. By coincidence, one house we were due to view in Chalfont St Giles fell through as we were en route, but another was offered, a fifteenth-century cottage called Old Beams in Threehouseholds, a road at the top of Chalfont St Giles leading to Seer Green. As soon as we saw it, I knew it would be a great place – one of the oldest cottages in the village (it had originally been a nursery school), coal-fired Aga, two staircases, two fires and superbly higgledy-piggledy. We put our deposit down and agreed to move in February.

Meanwhile, the Dutch company behind Body Glove had been back in touch, asking about our plans to launch the brand in the UK. They wanted to meet at a fashion exhibition in Cologne, Germany – on the day of our move. So, having hired a van, we packed up our belongings and one of Ann's brothers drove it to Chalfont St Giles while Ann went to work and I flew to Cologne to meet the Dutch Body Glove team.

It's amazing how much you can fit into your life if you have the appetite to do so. But you fit it in. You make it happen. You sort it out. Or, you do if you believe in what you're doing and that success is out there, somewhere.

In the meantime, I was still in touch with many of my friends from Portsmouth Poly and also the guys I'd met while at Haymarket Publishing and they all seemed to be doing really well in their lives and careers. 'Why don't you go back to advertising, Will?' they'd ask. 'You were really good at it.' 'That shaving oil you gave me, it's a bit greasy isn't it? I didn't like it at all. How do you think you can compete with Gillette? You're never going to get anywhere!' The fact that you are doing something different to your friends and peers can provoke quite a lot of resentment, especially if you seem to be enjoying what you're doing, while they may not be. Almost everyone I met, apart from my mum, dad, girlfriend, Herbie and Pat, thought I was crazy doing what I was doing and were certain that it wouldn't work.

The company I'd found to help with supplying the card for the shaving oil, Packaging Supplies, had been helpful in working with us on the Body Glove project too. Rob White, a young sales executive, helped us out. They provided storage for the samples while we worked out where to base the business; clearly it couldn't operate out of another bedroom in our new home.

Before moving to offices in Fleet Street, Herbie had a small serviced office suite on Fulham Road. One day we drove there to see what the cost of renting a room would be, with a receptionist who would answer the phone. The cost was reasonable, a few hundred pounds a month, so I decided to fit it out like a small clothing showroom, with rails to hang clothes on and the like. Consulting *Yellow Pages*, I tracked down a fashion wholesaler and shopfitter based in Tottenham and managed to buy some secondhand rails that I put up one afternoon. I turned a small boxroom into a showroom – well, in my eyes it was.

However, most of my thoughts were focused on the fast upcoming Boots meeting for King's King of Shaves. I'd prepared what I believed to be a good presentation about the product – why men would buy it and the fact that it was a tiny investment for Boots, which I believed would bring them substantial rewards. After all, there were about 1,300 Boots stores. I guessed from the 80/20 rule they'd do 80 per cent of their business out of about 300 stores. If Boots were prepared to order, say, 9 products per store (6 per store, 3 in the main warehouse), this would total 2,700 x £1.27 (my chosen wholesale price), an order of £3,429. Herbie had asked me to do a business plan for the oil, a sales projection as such, which I'd knocked out on a spreadsheet, and reckoned each store would sell one–two bottles per week. Therefore, annual sales could be around £40,000 – much more than the first year's sales, which were about £300 – not exactly a massive number. I had no idea whether £40,000 of projected sales in year one with a mass-market retailer was good or not (now I know most major retailers won't be interested in any brand that won't quickly get up to £1 million at retail!) but I guess ignorance was bliss.

The big day came quickly, and I drove up to Nottingham, getting more and more nervous as I got close to Boots' head office. Walking into the reception, the first thing that struck me was how many people were sitting there, mostly company sales representatives I guessed, and after signing in I sat there to wait. After about half an hour, the receptionist apologized that I'd had to wait and said Fiona would be with me shortly. Heart pounding, I skimmed through my presentation: 'King's, King of Shaves is a brand new way for men to shave without getting a painful rash or razor burn; it's attractively priced to you with a fifty per cent profit margin and the profit you'll make on every sale will be nearly equivalent to the sales price of the competition; I've got a really exciting press and publicity campaign planned to support the launch, by the PR agency who got Mr Blobby to number one at Christmas; I really believe that King's will fit extremely well at Boots. You're all about giving the customer great products with benefits, they trust Boots, and after enjoying King of Shaves, I know they'll come back and buy again.'

'Mr King? Fiona's ready to see you now.'

You're persistent, aren't you?

Yes. I know I've got a great product for you, and I really, really wanted you to be the first major retailer after Harrods to list it.

OK. Tell me about it.

[For the next fifteen minutes I launched into a presentation where I attempted to transfer all of my enthusiasm for King's, as I knew I almost certainly wouldn't get a second chance. We'd started the meeting almost forty minutes late, and I sensed that my time was coming to a close.]

How do I know it's going to sell?

Well, I've shaved with it every day for over a year now, and

*my skin is transformed. It used to be red, rashy and raw.
And now it's OK. I believe there are many men out there
who suffer from razor burn and I believe King's, the King of
Shaves can cure that. Customers will come back, they'll be
repeat purchasers and my dream of launching this shaving
oil with you will come true.*

OK. I'll be in touch.

When? I wanted to ask. Soon? But asking those questions
seemed to smack of desperation, so I bit my lip, thanked her
very much for taking the time to meet me, packed up my
samples, realized I hadn't put on my gold cardboard crown
(probably best I hadn't) and left. The meeting had lasted just
over fifteen minutes. I didn't know it then, but my life had just
changed.

As I write this, I've just finished a day in London, first of all
meeting the managing partner of a high-powered corporate
law firm, where over lunch we discussed what the next
three–four years will hold for King of Shaves. Herbie was with
me but had to return to the office, so I went to Boots' flagship
store on Oxford Street to check our brands, did a telephone
interview with Stephanie, a journalist at *Growing Business*
magazine for their awards issue (we were to be the cover story)
and then went for a final meeting with our ad agency, Hooper
Galton, to sign off the first national advertising campaign for
the Azor razor, due to kick off in April.

Life is full of T-junctions, where you have to stop, decide
which direction to take off in and go for it. At the Boots
meeting, this T-junction had a dead end and a road leading
somewhere. The point I make is that when you're in the midst
of setting up your business, your day will be full of T-junctions
and more often than not, roundabouts and dead ends. It's

vitally important to have a sort of navigation system in your mind where you can keep one eye on the direction you're travelling in and the other looking out for roadblocks, obstacles and, occasionally, short cuts. Every so often you must stop. Get away from the decision you're having to make. Give yourself a bit of breathing space. Impulsive and impetuous as I am sometimes, I do take stock of what is being said to me and, contrary to people's views, listen to them, take their views in and consider them carefully. Often, taking a break can stop you from making the wrong decision and ensure that the right decision can be found.

The Boots meeting was the culmination of months of preparation, which boiled down to fifteen minutes in which to convince a buyer, responsible for maybe £200 million of sales, that my single product, for which the opening order would be just £3,500, was going to change the sales and profit performance of her business, for the better. So, before you launch into your pitch, make sure you're prepared. As you'll have seen from watching *Dragon's Den*, there are no second chances.

As I was driving back from Boots, Herbie called to ask how it went. 'It went well,' I said.

'Got an order?'

'No, she said she'll be in touch.'

'Oh. Well done. I'm sure you gave it your best shot. See you!'

Truth be told, the meeting was an absolutely enormous anticlimax. I'd been firing myself up for it for months, it happened in a flash and I had no order.

'Onwards and upwards,' I thought to myself. March came and went, and I still hadn't heard from Boots. I was getting nervous. I was loath to pester them and I had no idea who the Boots CEO was. Even if I did, I wasn't going to invoke the

Harrods strategy again, that could be suicide.

Early April saw me starting to pull together the database of potential retailers for Body Glove and planning the summer sales campaign, where I'd be showing products to surf and fashion stores to sell in the autumn/winter season (this would be our first stab at sales as we hadn't had stock for spring/summer 1994). I resorted to trawling through surf, style and fashion magazines, looking for retail contacts and calling up the owners of the stores and asking them if they'd heard of Body Glove (many had) and if I could arrange to show them the range. They were a little more lukewarm about that.

Back in February I'd received a letter from Andy Hill, the chap who'd rented me the snowboard while I was on holiday in Val d'Isère. He was writing from Tignes, was returning to the UK soon and wondered if Body Glove might sponsor him next year. 'With what?' I thought to myself, looking daily at ever increasing outgoings and extremely small incomings. He wrote again and explained that he'd found meeting me really interesting and thought I might be a useful guy to stay in touch with. I was flattered and said I'd see him when he came back.

As well as meeting Andy when we were in Val d'Isère, Ann and I had also met a young guy called Julian. He'd had quite a go-getting attitude and was a good snowboarder too. My mind started to connect dots. Maybe I could get Julian to help me with Body Glove. He could stay with us (bit of an assumption without asking Ann), he'd get work experience, I'd get a helper and I could double up the workload on Body Glove.

I met Julian at the Body Glove 'showroom' in Fulham, showed him the sample collection, explained that the first range we'd be launching would be the autumn/winter collection (which was snowboarding jackets, winter jackets, fleeces, sweatshirts and the like) and asked whether he'd be interested in helping me. 'Love to. When can I start?'

'Can you drive?'

'Yes.'

'OK, well, I think you should talk with your mum [he was living at home] and if she's OK with it, you can live with us during the week to save on petrol and stay at home at the weekend.'

'Fine,' he said.

About a week later, I hadn't heard from him, so I called to find out what the problem was. 'Hi, you alright? Hadn't heard from you, is everything OK?'

'Um, not really. I've been banned from driving. I didn't want to tell you, as I thought I wouldn't get the job with you. Sorry.'

'Shit,' I thought to myself, 'what a pain.' 'Why were you banned?'

No answer. I didn't push.

'I'm in court next week, maybe you could pick me up afterwards and we can have a chat. I'd like to introduce you to my mum.'

'OK,' I said, and rang off. What was going on? From expecting to bring on a young work-experience helper, I was driving down to Reading Magistrates' Court to pick him up after his hearing.

I barely knew Julian, but I guess I agreed to meet him because I thought there was something in him that would be good to bring out further. This is a strength *and* a weakness in me. I've been known to hire a guy on the basis he sold electric razors at Boots and I've had one glass of wine too many and fired people who think I'm a soft touch (I rarely show any anger) to teach them a lesson (some of them have benefited greatly from being fired by me – they know who they are!). But having agreed to bring Julian aboard, it seemed wrong to just let him go when he was so obviously enthusiastic to work for me and felt his chance had gone. Giving people the chance and letting them fly (or not – it's not guaranteed!) is one of the great empowering satisfactions for a business owner or leader – well it is for me, anyway.

So, there I was, a surfwear brand and a shaving oil to sell, twin companies whose individual accounts needed managing, shareholders in both companies to keep updated, a couple of dogs to look after, a personal life to enjoy with my girlfriend and an aspiration that both businesses would be successful.

Product first, profit later

I'm writing this after enjoying a fantastic weekend with my dad, my brothers and our sons in Megève, a beautiful village at the foot of the French Alps, having flown there together on board a private jet. We skied during the day and in the evening enjoyed some great laughs with Dad, while mine and my brothers' kids had the time of their lives, Wii-ing when they weren't skiing.

Flying on a private jet is an experience far removed from commercial flying from a major airport. We were guests on this trip, no way does King of Shaves have a King Air arm, but it struck me how successful you have to be to travel in this way. After touching down at Farnborough earlier today, we taxied to our parking slot, which was one plane down from *Galactic Girl*, Sir Richard Branson's private jet. I managed to take a snap of it as we left as I know Will Whitehorn, the president of Virgin Galactic (he kindly came to the press launch for our Azor razor) and I'm booked to 'Go Galactic' in a couple of years or so (I'll explain why later (see page 277), but Sir Richard's trademark beard comes into it!).

If you've chosen to create a business, the only way people can generally judge its success is by how big it is or how much money you make – featuring in the *Sunday Times* Rich List, for example. Where King of Shaves is concerned, this has never been a prime motivating force for me, however. Sure, I'm aiming high. 'Head in space, feet on the ground' is how an article in the *Telegraph* described me, but I certainly don't spend every day thinking about how much money I'll make. What I do spend a huge amount of time thinking about is: 'How good are our products? Is our marketing effective? Is our company infrastructure working well? A few days prior to flying out to France I got an e-mail from Nicky Springle, my head of King of Shaves customer care, with the news that *Which?* magazine – the UK's leading independent consumer magazine – had voted our King of Shaves Azor a 'Best Buy' and 'Exceptional Value'. This is probably one of the most exciting pieces of product recognition we've had. We were up there with Gillette's Fusion Power and Mach3 Turbo. Even more telling was a pretty innocuous paragraph in the review which read:

The costs of using a shaving system

Replacing the blade cartridges for a shaving system can be expensive and, unlike printer cartridges, you won't be able to find cheap unbranded blades to attach to big-name razors. Manufacturers are keen to protect their razor innovations and Gillette have seventy patents on the Fusion alone. We found that the six shaving systems we tested had similar durability, but there were striking differences in cost. For example, when we checked, the Azor from King of

Shaves was half the price of the Gillette Fusion Power Stealth and came with three replacement blades, while the Power Stealth came with one. And buying a pack of four replacement blades for the Azor was half the price as well.

This was a hugely important review. This is market-disrupting stuff! A razor that delivers you a close, comfortable shave, but at 50 per cent cheaper than the competition. I had already blogged this fact and couldn't wait to post again. Getting this sort of good news out to the internet quickly is vital. If you are getting excited about setting up your business, you'd better become extremely conversant with how to use the web. Whether you use an online site that sells products and allows customers to post reviews, blog, tweet or use a social network like Facebook to target your ads, learning to use the internet to your advantage is an absolute priority. I'll be coming to how we came to own shave.com in a little while, but with my exhortation for you to concentrate on the product, not on making the money ringing in your ears, I'll take you back to spring 1994.

A 'Yes' from Boots

Having dropped off Ann for work as usual, I returned home to start my day of sales calls, administration, designing, thinking and generally getting on with stuff. It wasn't until midday when I was due to walk Moke and Dud, that I realized I hadn't checked the post. There was a white envelope with a Boots logo on it. And it was quite thick.

I ripped it open, expecting it to be from Fiona, but it was from the supplier team saying that Knowledge & Merchandising Inc. Ltd was to be set up as a Boots supplier and they needed all manner of details from me, from a VAT number to banking details, references and more. There was also quite an onerous form to fill in regarding product liability insurance and other information. It sank in. There was *no way* that they'd be setting KMI up as a supplier if they weren't going to list King of Shaves.

Yes!

Using the WinFax PRO programme on my computer, I quickly wrote Fiona a thank-you letter with a funny cover page (including a picture of a man standing on top of the world), faxed it off to her office number and went out to walk the dogs. When I came back, I had a fax reply that ran to a couple of lines, advising me that Boots would be trialling King's in several hundred stores and that I should expect their opening order within a couple of weeks.

I rang Herbie and Ann to tell them the news and having then taken myself off into the garden for a smoke and a little walk and talk to myself, came back indoors thinking of all the stuff that needed to be done.

When I read through the supplier information document again, I realized that Boots expected me to use a system called Electronic Data Interchange (EDI) to receive orders on, which of course I didn't have (and it also seemed to cost a lot of money), so I rang the supply team at Boots and explained my predicament. I was a small, single-product (or stock-keeping unit (SKU)) supplier, I had no knowledge about EDI and was there a different way we could receive orders? I was asked to hold for what seemed like ages, sat in my old chair in front of my cheap IKEA desk thinking 'What if they say I *have* to have EDI? How can we afford it?' After five minutes or so someone came back on the line and said that as I was such a small supplier and it appears that King's is only being trialled (my heart sort of sank a bit at this phrase) then they'd be able to fax me my order (normally weekly, on a Thursday) and in my completed supplier pack I needed to include a fax number that they could reach me at.

Let me tell you, in business, there's always a hill or mountain to climb and it never gets any easier. The complexity of essentially me supplying Boots was starting to increase. Remember, I had done pretty much everything myself and when I wasn't working on King of Shaves I was making sure we had a database of surfwear shops to visit with Body Glove or that the bank accounts were in credit or that I was on top of the (albeit tiny) invoices that were being raised.

The ability to work hard and not give up, ever, must be something that every single successful entrepreneurial businessperson has to have. From Alan Sugar to Richard Branson, you start off pretty much on your own and when you simply can't do it all any more you have to scale the business. That means hiring people; people you probably can't afford to pay yet (but you'll find a way) and they must be good people at that. Although Julian was helpful and enthusiastic, he would essentially do what I asked him to do, which meant me spending a lot of my time explaining tasks to him, which he'd dutifully and effectively carry out. However, he wouldn't necessarily take the initiative.

While mobile phones were useful for keeping in touch, nowhere near as much business was done on them in the early/mid-1990s as is done today. One of my bugbears was being tied to a phone in a room and one of the earliest investments I made was in a couple of Rabbit phones (some of you may remember these, they were digital phones that would work near a base station, these were located in post offices, banks, etc., but when you were out of range they'd be useless;

they were a sort of early Wi-Fi phone). Now at least when people or companies rang KMI or Core Brands I didn't have to be sitting at my desk to answer! Today, all my staff at King of Shaves have digital cordless phones so they can roam the building at will. This might be a small thing, but trust me, the ability to hold a telephone conversation while standing in a different room potentially allows you to take control of a business conversation, where if you are wired to a desk, with others around, it's not so easy.

I recall the next few weeks being pretty frantic, making sure that the outers of King of Shaves were ready to be shipped from the contract packer/deliverer, that my (single) barcode scanned properly, that I understood about pallet heights and more. It was manic. I was twenty-nine, had no experience of male grooming or surf fashion and was making most of it up as I went along. But it was great fun!

As the day for my first ever Boots order drew closer, I realized that I had to get some publicity for the King's, King of Shaves shaving revolution launch! I'd had a little bit of press coverage and some nice letters from the few men who'd actually bought the oil. One was from a Mr Mel Rockett, who wrote me a delightful letter explaining how pleased he was with the oil and could he buy some more by mail order?

There was so much to get done. I knew there was no way Herbie could join me at this stage because of his other commitments. Julian was mainly helping to get all the details in order for the first sample shipment of Body Glove clothing and unless I looked after King's, it didn't get done.

Another letter arrived from Andy Hill, asking if there was any chance of sponsorship for the forthcoming season. I called him and asked him to come to the house and look at all the 1993–4 autumn/winter samples. I said I'd sponsor him with

£1,500 worth of clothing if he agreed to mention Body Glove in his upcoming season. I vividly remember sitting with Andy in the front room of Old Beams and going through the clothes that might actually be of use to him or that he'd wear! He's a medium-built, very fit, wiry chap and the big problem was that all of the samples were in two sizes, large and extra large! Anyhow, we managed to find a few items that were of use and he made lots of comments about how the clothing could be improved, which I passed back to the Dutch team (which no doubt went straight into their shredder!). Andy and I next crossed paths in spring 1995.

Early May came and still no order from Boots. I started feeling nervous, so I called Fiona. 'Hi, hope you're well, I'm really looking forward to the first order . . . any idea when we'll have it?'

'Will, you have to be the most persistent, tenacious person ever!' she said laughing. 'It'll be with you on Thursday.'

That same day, instead of walking the dogs through the woods, I went into Chalfont St Giles and had a drink at the Merlin's Cave. On the way back I realized that I needed to get some photocopying done and as I was thinking about this I walked past a door front on which was a sign saying 'Chiltern House – office administration services within'. I'd never noticed it before, so I tied up the dogs by the butcher's and went in. A nice young lady called Emma explained to me that they provided office services – sending and receiving faxes, photocopying and answering phone calls (i.e. if I was out I could redirect the call to their number and they'd answer on my behalf). What a result! I asked how much the services cost and she explained that there was a small monthly charge but after this their services were on a per use basis. 'Great,' I thought to myself, – 'if I'm not in I can redirect the fax and phone number there, and have myself a "virtual office".'

Emma said she'd seen me walking my dogs and wondered what I did as I was around the village a bit. 'Setting up a shaving and surfwear business.' I said. 'I'll get some for your boyfriend or dad to try.'

She laughed. 'OK, see you soon!'

I had my first proper employee, she just didn't work 100 per cent for me yet!

I used to think things always took about six times longer to get done than they should and I still think that today, even with the speed of the internet. It sometimes takes ages for things to happen and this is a huge issue with a start-up business when you're trying to build momentum. It's especially an issue in a product-based business. Products have to be designed, made, warehoused and shipped. They have to be bought by someone, used and, hopefully, and this is mission critical, rebought. Otherwise it is all in vain.

This is why so many companies and products fail. They go through all of the points mentioned above but with an average, or undifferentiated product and wonder why it hasn't worked. Let's get one thing straight. It's *all* about the product or service.

The million-dollar home page

My favourite example of a great business idea well executed is Alex Tew's milliondollarhomepage.com. If you don't know what it is check it out, it's still live, but here's a quick explanation. Alex needed to raise some money to go to university and had already developed a couple of internet businesses that hadn't worked out. The money that should have taken him through uni was rapidly running out and he hadn't even got there yet!

In early 2005 he had the brainwave of building a site where the page on screen would be split into pixels and each group of pixels would be sold for $10 (you'd have to spend $100 to actually see your ad). You could advertise absolutely anything (legal), you could pay using PayPal and could own your own piece of internet history.

The site started off pretty low-key, he got a few mates to sign up and a little bit of word of mouth going, but, nothing spectacular. Then in late spring, early summer of 2005, the site started to be talked about on blogs. By early autumn, Alex's idea had been featured in a major US national newspaper. I saw the article and immediately visited the site. It was still a work in progress at the time, lots of white space interspersed with logos and 'click heres'. I read his blog and, amazingly for me, didn't buy a set of pixels for the King of Shaves brand. Big mistake.

Publicity around the site skyrocketed and at one stage it was in the top half a dozen visited sites on the internet. Sure, it was a completely random site – if someone clicked on a brand logo it was unlikely they'd have anything in common with the brand – but as an awareness vehicle it was phenomenal. I kicked myself for not getting our brand on it and by way of self-consolation I dropped Alex an e-mail congratulating him on his success and wondered if I could send him some King of Shaves product. He e-mailed back almost immediately, 'I already use it – great brand,' he said.

Since the original site, there have been literally tens of thousands of sites all doing exactly the same as Alex's did. None has succeeded. Why? Because why would anyone want to visit them, let alone pay to advertise on them? Alex's idea was unique and a one-off. Thinking about setting up a new business? Your business must have a USP. If it doesn't, it's dead.

The first order from Boots

Just after 3 p.m. on Thursday 12 May 1994, my very first order from Boots arrived. For immediate delivery, it was due to be in-store by 24 May. It was for 2,700 units of King's, King of Shaves 10-ml Original Shaving Oil at a unit price of £1.27 excluding VAT, £4,029.08 including VAT.

Wow!

From the placement of that first order, I didn't look back. I knew in my heart of hearts that people would enjoy using the product, that it had a homemade quirkiness about it that would invite examination and curiosity and because I shaved with it every day and it worked for me it would work for others. I had 100 per cent faith in it. What I didn't realize was how long it would take to build meaningful sales momentum.

As the product wasn't going to be on sale for another couple of weeks, I had no reorders. The terms of business with Boots were 2.5 per cent settlement discount for payment at the end of the month following invoice. I had invoiced as soon as the product was delivered but then realized that I had to wait until the end of June to get any money in!

'Turnover is vanity, profit is sanity, cash is king' the saying goes. In my case cash flow was king, and I had none of it, let alone any cash. I'd depleted my 10,000 bottles by 2,700 and had no idea what repeat orders would follow (would one, two or ten bottles sell per store per week?). I couldn't really face another two weeks bottling again, so I had to quickly turn my mind to building stock (or dead cash, as it's called in our business).

Getting serious about business

Inventory control, stock holding and pipefill were all phrases that soon entered my vocabulary, as I started to evolve KMI from a one-off producer into a manufacturer of a product of consistent quality. Because I now had Boots as a stockist, people who'd previously been unwilling to contract supply to me started to change their tune. The company that had supplied the shaving oil bulk agreed to fill 10,000 units on their line, I was able to negotiate 30 days' credit with Measom Freer and they were able to help me find a new bottle printer. So, my home wouldn't be invaded by 10,000 oil bottles again! This sort of business I now routinely describe as virtually integrated. We own everything (the brand) yet nothing (no physical manufacture). This is very much the only way you can safely start up a product-based business. I needed and wanted to work with the best manufacturing partners and largely this is still the case today.

As with any task, when you've done it once and you're reasonably bright, you get better at doing it. After a while, what looks to others to be incredibly complex simply becomes second nature to you. By using this principle of virtual integration I was able to control the King of Shaves brand (its look, feel, appearance) and relinquish control of the physical manufacture to talented others, with of course terms and conditions attached.

I'd told my mum and dad to look out for King of Shaves in their local Boots and in early June took a phone call from my dad. 'Hey Will, I've been into Boots and bought the King of Shaves – well done!'

But I hadn't had a repeat order and was starting to get nervous all over again. As you are reading this, you'll probably notice one recurrent letter – 'I'. *I* did this. *I* made that. *I* packed. *I* posted. *I* called. *I* thought. *I* designed. And *I* did. Herbie had a day job. Ann was working in London. The dogs weren't that hot on the computer, so they lived a dog's life. And that left me.

There's a well-known saying that 'There's no "I" in team', but I tell you something, there's definitely an 'I' in 'leader'. Only one person can lead and you must recognize that the success of any business that you set up or create rests fairly and squarely with you. When I look back on the early days I realize that in the hundreds, no, thousands of days you personally spend doing the vast majority of stuff yourself are absolutely the most valuable days spent. Experience cannot be bought, it can only be earned, and there is no substitute for it.

Indeed, if I haven't bored you and you've got this far, it may be well worth taking the time to see if you have the belief in yourself to actually start (or finish) something – that unpainted back bedroom, that photo album waiting to be filled, planning that hiking holiday you've always wanted to have, but never got round to. I talked earlier in the book about how starting is the single most difficult thing to do. And it is. Because it's you who has to do it. It's your responsibility.

Drawing on my experience of the early days of KMI, I look at the tasks my talented staff now do, things I once did, and I know how well they are (or aren't) coping. The stresses and strains inherent in their jobs were once inherent in mine. If I was able to get the job done to the best of my ability, then there is no reason why they shouldn't be able to achieve the same.

But make no mistake, this is an 'I' book, a book you must read with you in mind and no one else.

There is an 'I' in Tigger and there definitely isn't in Eeyore.

Chapter 11: Building a Brand

All I remember about the remainder of 1994 (apart from the disappointment of watching a World Cup without an England team being present) was working incredibly hard. Summer was taken up by a four-week tour around the UK in a rented white van along with Julian, visiting owners of surf shops. We set up racks of clothing, met dozens of potential Body Glove stockists, took their details and their orders for the autumn/winter range (which many weren't interested in) and just kept on going.

Every time we stopped at a hotel or guesthouse, I would connect my computer to a phone line, activate WinFax Pro and see if we had an order for King of Shaves from Boots. If we did, I'd send off an instruction to the freight company to get it shipped and prepare an invoice using Quicken, the personal finance package.

It wasn't an easy time at home. I'd now been pretty much immersed in the business for over two years and it's fair to say my relationship with Ann was strained, although we managed to keep it on the rails.

We got £30–40,000 worth of orders for Body Glove – one particularly big order was from the buyer of a company called Free Spirit, who ordered just under £10,000 worth of goods – but generally getting retailers interested was hard. The Dutch company behind Body Glove were pressing us to sign a quite onerous distribution agreement, with minimum purchase quantities, commitments to market spends, etc. That company had its own working-capital requirements, and although it wasn't competing with King of Shaves, Body Glove did compete for my time. In many ways, Body Glove won the battle. Most people, because they knew the brand, thought it would be successful. Others, who had no shaving problems at all, ridiculed King of Shaves. King of Shaves was netting orders of 300 to 600 bottles per week, with a few hundred pounds being invoiced on a regular basis, whereas Body Glove *promised* sales of tens of thousands, even if the reality was actually quite different. I enjoyed both businesses; both were quite 'cool' in their own way, but I guess I always maintained a fondness for King of Shaves as it was the business I'd started from scratch.

Using publicity to bring the brand alive

I touched on the importance of the oxygen of publicity earlier in the book. Indeed, one of the main reasons, if not *the* reason I'm writing this is to bring King of Shaves as a brand alive to you, in the same way we needed to bring King of Shaves alive to the consumers via media coverage. But how?

Brian MacLaurin's company, MacLaurin Communications, was starting to gather its own momentum and I'd asked if he would consider taking an equity stake in KMI in return for a press and publicity campaign. He politely explained that he couldn't, for, as much as he knew he could do a great job, he needed hard cash.

I got hold of Pat Maris and asked if he knew anyone who might consider investing so that we could raise money for PR. 'Try my brother Antony,' he said. 'I've talked to him about what I've invested in, but he's completely different to me, and will want to meet Herbie and you.'

So, we met Antony in a wine bar in Victoria, London, and explained what we needed more money for. 'Basically,' I said, 'we need to run a national PR campaign about King's. I have just the chap who's prepared to do it, it's a six-month campaign and it's going to cost about ten thousand pounds. We're prepared to offer you ten per cent of KMI for ten thousand pounds. What do you think?'

Antony is a pretty serious chap and rightly asked lots of questions. He was a senior executive in the oil business and about to start an MBA at Kingston University. I had Herbie with me and we were both able to reassure him that regular sales (albeit small) were coming in from Boots, that I was now able to set up meetings with other retailers like Superdrug and Tesco and that we definitely had repeat sales. Antony agreed to invest.

I met Brian the following week to discuss our press offensive. 'Will,' he said, 'there are two parts to making this a success. You and the product. In fact, you are the product. People don't want to read about an oil that may or may not improve their daily scrape, what they want to read about is a story, something they can relate to and believe in. Something they can get behind. They want to relate to you as David battling the Goliaths of the shaving industry. They need to know what you've gone through, are going through. Leave it with me, I'll get you my proposal.' A week or so later, a sheaf of typewritten paper arrived at Old Beams, along with a retainer fee note of £10,000, payable monthly in arrears. It's worth hearing from Brian himself at this point:

> *Will and I met at a pivotal moment in both our careers. I had just joined a young consultancy after twenty years as a corporate employee and Will King, a*

somewhat fresher-faced, younger man than me, was breaking out into a marketing consultancy from a more mundane job in sales. Fortunately for both of us the companies we had joined fell victim to the recession of the early 1990s and since those days we have progressed to greater things in our own fields.

On meeting it was clear Will was an obsessively driven young man with a firm belief that in life anything is possible. He positively bubbled with excitement as he confronted each and every task. Will had a propensity to challenge the norm and did everything in an entirely unexpected way.

But I also saw a very different side to Will. Here was someone who was clearly ambitious and apparently oozing confidence, but he quickly showed to me that he was also vulnerable. Within months of meeting him, he asked me for guidance, slightly tongue in cheek, as to what he needed to do in image terms to get to the top. I was a little shocked as I saw a tear emerge from the corner of his eye when I responded, 'You will need to get your teeth fixed first.'

It may sound cruel, but I was making a genuine point. Why pitch for business, talk to your bankers or meet suppliers and have them focusing on your teeth? Needless to say Will took my advice and he has ribbed me about it ever since, announcing to everyone new he introduces me to that I am the only man that has made him cry!

I started MacLaurin Communications in 1993 immediately after the marketing consultancy we had joined had collapsed. My new business had been running for only two months when Will called and asked for a meeting. He told me he wanted to start a company selling a new shaving oil to avoid shaving rash, something he had knocked up in his sink. Of course, I always thought he was a little mad, but surely he was completely insane when he suggested I take ownership of 10 per cent of the shares in his business in return for free PR consultancy to promote his new product.

He wasn't joking, but I told him he should keep his shares, and I definitely needed the income to pay my staff. Confidently, he told me he would be back in a month. Sure enough he returned having sold shares to a friend to raise the necessary cash to hire my fledgling agency to promote his new brand. A full-scale PR campaign then got underway.

It was at this time that I'd come to realize that more and more people referred to King's as King of Shaves. However, I was still not confident enough to drop the King's name (especially as this was how Boots bought it and how it was stickered on the shelf) so I kept it on the pack, although I started referring to the product as King of Shaves or KoS, not King's.

Setting up shop for Body Glove

With the sales season for selling Body Glove having ended, we had a couple of hundred garments that were surplus to requirements. (We knew we'd shortly be asked to buy more stock and were planning to exhibit the new lines at a clothing exhibition at the GMEX centre in Manchester.) There was simply no place to put them. The small serviced office room in London was already overflowing with garments and there was definitely no place for them at home, even though I'd managed to store quite a few boxes upstairs in the loft.

Herbie lived in Chesham. I explained to him that we had all these clothes, many of which were perfectly saleable, and asked what we might do with them. 'Why don't we sell them?' he said. 'There are some shops in Chesham that could be available. I know a commercial property chap who could find out what's available for us.' Before I knew it, I was visiting small shops on Chesham's pedestrianized high street, with a view to opening a surfwear shop!

After visiting a couple of properties we looked at one that was near the town clock and square that looked suitable. The rent was about £15,000 a year. It needed completely refurbishing but it had some good storage space at the rear, with parking too. 'In for a penny, in for a pound,' I thought, and agreed with Herbie that we'd take it on a two-year lease with a year break. 'Over to you,' he said and I realized that I now had to open a shop!

Not having any idea of what this involved, the gutting and refurbishment of a premises is quite an undertaking, I just got on with it. I spent days stripping and skipping the rubbish inside it. I sanded the floors with an industrial floor sander (I quite enjoyed that). I also decided that covering up the walls with sheets of corrugated iron would look quite urban and cool, chose a colour scheme and asked my dad if he'd stay for a week and help me paint the outside of the shop. I found a security shutter, went to Costco to buy a small TV and video, got a lot of hanging rails from the shop in Tottenham and even found a six-foot glass aquarium to display fish in. No business plan or profit and loss projection was drawn up for the shop. All I knew was that I had around £15,000 worth of kit to sell, with the next delivery of stock imminent. I kidded myself that it would be a great market-research tool to see what would sell and use that knowledge in our ongoing sales process for Body Glove. Julian was appointed store manager.

People would walk up and down Chesham high street wondering what the shop was going to be. 'A butcher's' my dad would quip to passers-by or 'Wait and see!' For some reason, I decided to call the shop $uss'd and found a black-smith in Beaconsfield to design a nice sign. As we had some women's clothing too, I had a small sign designed that read $uss'd Sister.

While I was doing this I was effectively running KMI *and* Core Brands (Body Glove) from the shop. I had temporarily moved my computer to the store, redirected the fax line so I could receive orders and Emma was answering calls for KMI if I wasn't at home.

Getting column inches for King of Shaves

I'd been to see Brian a couple of times to explain how things were going with King of Shaves. He'd asked that I get a photo done of me holding the product and he wanted to meet his new account executive, a young lady called Sophie Rhys-Jones. Yes, now the Countess of Wessex, Prince Edward's wife! Sophie seemed enthusiastic about King of Shaves and genuinely excited to be working on the account. Brian explained that he had a number of irons in the fire and that he would be in touch in the next week or so. Here, Brian MacLaurin explains a publicity stunt involving the future Countess of Wessex:

By the mid-1990s, the MacLaurin agency had an eclectic client base, including Noel Edmonds, Chris Tarrant, numerous radio stations, Chrysalis records and was also undertaking a brief project for HRH Prince Edward. On the payroll of the agency was a young Sophie Rhys-Jones. During a photo session with Prince Edward I introduced Sophie to him and the rest, as they say, is history.

Sophie found herself regularly in the media and Will definitely spotted an opportunity. I noticed that whenever he was talking about his PR agency, the MacLaurin reference slowly disappeared and Will would say that Sophie Rhys-Jones was running the King of Shaves PR account.

One of the many MacLaurin scams for King of Shaves in the early days was to pack commuter trains (completely illegally) with businessmen with briefcases. After the train pulled out from the station these men opened their briefcases, donned an ermine robe, placed a crown on their heads and went about distributing trial bottles of King of Shaves. The impact was huge. However, we were caught and Will made sure that the resultant potentially negative publicity carefully linked the future wife of Prince Edward to

> *the idea that had so upset British Rail. King managed*
> *a true royal connection!*

True to his word, Brian was working on something for me and came up with a stunning piece of press coverage, probably the most important I've ever had. I was to feature in the *Mail on Sunday*'s *You* magazine, complete with a photo and the promise that 'If they like you, they might look at doing a whole page!' The interview was to be published on 1 January 1995.

Wow! Within a couple of weeks I was in a photo studio, with a make-up artist and photographer, having my picture taken sitting astride a barber's chair. After the photo shoot I was interviewed by a lady called Lisa Markwell. After the interview ended I asked her who else she was interviewing. 'Well, funny you should ask that Will. I can't tell you who I'm interviewing next, but I recently interviewed Julia Carling, Will Carling's wife [then captain of the England rugby team] and mentioned I was interviewing the guy behind King of Shaves shaving oil. "I buy that for Will," she said, "he likes it!"'

I was gobsmacked.

Superdrug had been high on my hit list since signing Boots and in late November I heard that they were to trial King's in twenty-five stores. Excellent.

The grand opening of $uss'd

On a rainy winter's day in early December 1994, we held our grand opening of $uss'd. We'd even managed to get a celebrity to open it, an actor called Dave Glover, then a big star in *Emmerdale*. We managed to convince Dave to wear a wetsuit and hold a Body Glove surfboard, and we got some coverage from the local newspapers.

Initial trade was quite brisk and I felt quite good about the shop. The fact that somehow, along with Herbie, Julian and other friends and family, we'd been able to open a store, and also find a way for Julian to earn some money, was very satisfying.

I was there the week after opening when Brian called. 'Will, I've got the *Daily Express* interested in running a piece on you – David v Goliath – you should expect a call from a journalist in the next hour or so. Here's what you have to say.' He explained to me how to talk to the press and what they were interested in. The idea was to ensure the press felt there was a good story in the interview and not just talk about how great King of Shaves shaving oil was, but focus on the start-up story behind it. 'Don't confuse them with what you're doing with Body Glove,' he said. 'Just tell them how you were made redundant, you needed to get a job, you didn't like shaving, you used an oil, see where it goes.' Within a short time I took a call from Helen Slingsby, and spent about half an hour talking to her. 'When might it be published?' I asked. 'Next week, hopefully,' she said. 'Good luck.'

And so, on 19 December 1994 I got my first piece of national press coverage – 'Nicking a soothing shaving niche'. On 1 January 1995, I rushed down to the newsagent, bought the *Mail on Sunday* and hurriedly leafed through *You* magazine. There it was. A full page. 'Will King – Young blade in business'. What a start to the new year!

My brush with a conman

A week or so after the *You* magazine piece had been published,

I took a call from a man who wanted to take me to lunch and discuss the future of King of Shaves. I asked who he was and he said he was connected and had a proposal to put to me.

With the businesses consuming ever more cash, I was intrigued, as maybe he would be a potential investor who could come in alongside us and help accelerate the sales of the brand. Superdrug were making noises about extending their distribution, I'd managed to meet Sainsbury's and had a meeting with Tesco planned in April. I knew I'd need to build more stock and the invoices from Boots, although regularly paid, were not even close to keeping us on top of our working capital requirement.

The lunch was surreal. The chap was quite elderly, apparently intrigued by the brand, the way I was marketing it and its potential. 'I have a good friend who is in the fragrance business,' he explained. 'We'd like to see if we could be your international distributor.' I'm quite a trusting chap by nature and was flattered by his interest in the business. It was a strange meeting however, something didn't seem right, but I put my misgivings to the back of my mind and we arranged to meet up again in London, where he would introduce me to some of his contacts. Having paid for lunch, he left.

I was soon to learn there is no such thing as a free lunch.

Under pressure

As the businesses grew I had to spend more and more time on a huge number of tasks just to keep my head above water. When I wasn't at $uss'd seeing how Julian was doing, I'd be out with a supplier, trying to get hold of a retailer, dealing with the increasing amounts of correspondence with the Body Glove team in Holland, keeping the company accounts up to date, dealing with VAT, etc. By mid-February I was completely exhausted. I couldn't carry on working literally twenty-four seven. What had been fun was getting on top of me and I realized that something had to change otherwise I'd make a big mistake – overlook something or not be on top of the situation.

I called Herbie. 'H, can we meet? I need to talk to you.' We met the next day at a beautiful old pub called The Swan at Ley Hill, near Chesham. Pints ordered, I got straight to the point. 'Herb, I can't cope at the moment. I've got too much on, too many plates spinning, and I'm afraid something's going to give and it might be me. What can we do?' Herbie, with an MBA from INSEAD and years of consulting experience, knew that it was time to make a decision regarding KMI and Core Brands. He'd been running the Smile business, which had by now opened a second outlet near Bexley Heath, but didn't seem to be enjoying it much. 'I guess it's time we worked together on these businesses,' he said. 'I can see you've got way too much on and I know you need help.'

'What will you do about money?' I asked.

'I don't know, we'll work something out. Let's decide what next week,' he replied.

I'm not too sure what would have happened if I hadn't shared with Herbie my fears, concerns and worries about the business. Sharing your shortcomings, as well as your successes, is important to build a bond of trust in a business. No one is right all the time and I was pleased I'd outlined my worries and even more pleased that Herbie appeared willing to join me. 'I'll get another desk in the bottom room of Old Beams,' I said.

'Will, there's no way I'm working with you there, as much as I like you! We'll have to get an office locally. Can you see if you can find one?'

Finding your USP

Back to the present day. We've just announced our first national advertising campaign for King of Shaves and Azor, based around our patented Technology of Bendology™, the flexible head innovation on the Azor.

There's a great book you should read called *Zag* by Marty Neumeier. It's about the power of brand differentiation. (I came across it only after describing our business as 'zagging when others zig' in an interview in April 2008.) It's a very thought-provoking read and I can see much of King of Shaves's market approach over the past sixteen years in it.

For example, it asks you to describe your product (or brand) in one sentence, pulling out a core USP:

Our _____ is the only _____ that _____.

The sentence for our Azor would be:

Our <u>razor</u> is the only <u>razor</u> that <u>bends</u>.

The sentence for our first shaving product would be:

Our <u>shaving product</u> is the only <u>shaving product</u> that's <u>made from oil</u>.

You see where I'm coming from? You must have a uniqueness that allows you to highlight a core feature and benefit to the consumer.

Trademark denied

In early March I was shocked to hear from the UK Patent Office in response to my application for the registered trademark 'King of Shaves' in Class 3. The UK Patent and Trademark Office wrote, 'We view King of Shaves as a laudatory mark, and accordingly it is refused,' was the essence of the letter. 'What?' I said to myself. 'Why?'

During the past sixteen years I've spent a lot of time working on what's called intellectual property (IP). It's very important. If you own a ® after your brand name, it means no one else can use that word in the context of a competitive (or non-competitive) product. King of Shaves now owns many trademarks – Shaving Software® for example, along with Shaving Hardware®, Wash Through Index® and Azor®. But we weren't able to own King of Shaves®.

I had personally applied for the registration and had obviously underestimated the process. My reasoning was that my name is King, I'm selling my shaving product, so calling it King of Shaves must be fine. Wrong. A laudatory mark implies the product is the best of its genre and is rarely granted. One example, gained over many years of manufacturing and market growth, is Budweiser – King of Beers®. There was no way I could contemplate not owning King of Shaves as a trademark. What if other competitors started claiming their shaving product was the king of shaves? In my mind, we would lose our differentiation and uniqueness.

I returned to the patent research library at Southampton Row and asked about firms who might help me in getting this decision examined. There was a handbook in the foyer and I leafed through it. 'Marks & Clerk – the UK's leading Trademark and Patent Attorneys' caught my eye. I made an appointment to see a lady called Katherine Sutcliffe the following week; this was one hurdle that needed dealing with urgently.

Owning trademarks and patents is a valuable (although

intangible) addition to your company's balance sheet. By intangible, I mean that as they don't physically exist any bank or lender automatically disregards them as they don't represent any tangible value. Although I regard ownership of the King of Shaves and Azor trademarks as massively valuable – £50 million upwards – this amount can only be used as borrowing collateral when the same amount of cash is paid for them. It's a bit like having to sell the family silver to realize its value: the silver has a value already of course, but it appears invisible to the lender.

To cut a long story short, I was emphatic that there was no way that I couldn't be allowed to register the King of Shaves trademark and after quite a few heated meetings with Marks & Clerk they set off on a mission to argue my case. They seemed optimistic it could be resolved but the whole process would have to be started again from scratch and it would cost from £3–5,000, 'depending on how much resistance we run into', Katherine explained. 'More expense,' I thought. Katherine and her colleagues worked out a simple strategy that not being able to use my name in the context of selling my product was a breach of my rights; i.e. had my name been Smith, then Smith of Shaves would be fine, but because I had the surname King, there should be no reason why it shouldn't be King of Shaves. Finally we won through and after three years of trying we were able to put King of Shaves® on the packaging.

However, owning brand names with ™ and ® after them is only half the battle. The other half is people knowing about them, buying them, trying them and repeat purchasing. Putting your product on the shelf is one thing, you will get a certain amount of sales simply by people browsing, perhaps being curious about something new and giving it a go. But the oxygen of publicity, the persuasion of an endorsement or TV ad, will bring your product to a whole new set of people. Somehow, you have to leverage your brand using any means necessary, and in 1995 the business had already invested £10,000 in a publicity campaign that had got the brand and me into the national press. But this was nowhere near enough to give it a growth momentum. What else could I do to increase awareness? 'Why not sign Will Carling to endorse King of Shaves?' I thought to myself, 'Why not?'

Getting Will Carling to endorse King of Shaves

I got on the phone to Brian and asked him if he could find out who Will's agent was. The answer was the sports agent, Jon Holmes, based up in Nottingham. I phoned Jon Holmes and was asked to send a fax explaining my proposal regarding Will and was told Jon would get back to me. Please bear in mind here that KMI was on its way to *increasing* losses from the £30,000 posted in year one to a further £70,000 in year two, although sales turnover was up to £58,000 from £300. But to finance any deal with a leading rugby star we'd definitely need more money. I eyed my bank statements, credit-card bills and loan agreements with a wary eye. I'd already had my Amex card refused in a local restaurant due to late payment of the bill. I wondered how much Will would cost.

'Try and Convert, I Did' was the slogan I had in my mind that would announce Will Carling's involvement with King of Shaves – on the pack, in publicity material and hopefully via a new-fangled invention early adopters were getting excited about called the internet. In 1995 most people were unaware of the internet or the world wide web. I'd come across it only in reading marketing and technology magazines, and mainly because of the launch of companies like Compuserve and AOL.

Compuserve, which was then one of the biggest internet service providers (ISPs), was particularly interesting as part of its subscription model allowed you online access to information from a variety of sources, so I could access information on trademarks and intellectual property. I got an email address for KMI – 100437.75@compuserve.com. I proudly displayed our new electronic address on the bottom of our letterhead – how cutting edge were we? I also spent more time reading about the internet and what it might mean to a brand like King of Shaves.

Jon Holmes came back to me in late March with a simple three-page proposal for Will Carling to endorse King of Shaves. It was a three-year deal, from April 1995 to April 1998, and involved KMI paying Will a retainer that increased over the term (back-weighted to later years, as I had explained to John that we were a tiny brand, but that we would be big) and a percentage of sales from packs that bore his image and signature.

Brian was excited about the deal. I'm not at all sure he thought it would happen – after all, Will was a huge rugby star in 1995, very high profile and about to go to the Rugby World Cup. But, I thought I had a chance, he used King of Shaves, money was money and rugby players earned nowhere near the endorsement fees that football players earned (as we found out when we signed John Terry to endorse King of Shaves from April 2006 to June 2008, see page 255).

The contract came through from Jon dated 1 April. I didn't want to sign this deal on April Fool's Day, that seemed to be tempting fate a bit, so I asked for it to be dated a day later. On the transfer to Jon of £8,000, the deal was done. This was a huge gamble for the brand: our sales were just shy of £60,000;

our profit margin was about 25 per cent at this time, way too low and with all the other money we'd spent on publicity, marketing, trademarks and the like, the loss on these sales was big. I put it to the back of my mind. Here's Brian MacLaurin's take on the deal:

Will King has the luck of the devil, although he would argue it is a case of him being 'far sighted'. When he suggested to me that he would like us to secure the services of Will Carling (as it turned out, the first man to captain England in a Rugby World Cup final), as the face of his brand and revealed the paltry budget available, I advised there was little chance.

However, not only did Will Carling agree to the proposal, and then come to my office, remove his shirt and be photographed on the main floor of the agency, to the thrill of the female staff, but within months the profile of Carling escalated dramatically when allegations began to circulate that he had been travelling in and out of Kensington Palace in the boot of a car as his friendship with Princess Diana had supposedly blossomed.

Over the following months, with Carling's picture on all King of Shaves packaging, there was certainly only one winner!

Tesco get on board

In mid-April 1995, two years after setting up, we moved into a small boxroom of an office at Stone House, above a supermarket in Chalfont St Giles. It was cheap, convenient, had a lovely water meadow over the road where I could walk the dogs at lunchtime and, best of all, it was a base for the businesses. To celebrate, I designed a brass company plaque that I lovingly placed outside the access door. It read: 'Knowledge & Merchandising Inc. Ltd Home of the King of Shaves™'.

I immediately faxed all the buyers explaining we had signed the England rugby captain, Will Carling, to endorse King of Shaves with the slogan *'Try and Convert, I Did'* and was rewarded with an invitation to visit Tesco and present King of Shaves to them, something that had so far eluded me. The meeting went well. I had mocked up a new pack with Carling's face on it, had finally dropped 'King's', changed the colourway to a lighter blue, made 'King of Shaves' big and added the 'Try and Convert' slogan on to the front of the pack.

We had another stockist.

Leverage

Let me talk a little more about leverage. You have to make consumers aware of your company, product or brand in the biggest way possible. Confidence breeds confidence. Where the retailers were concerned, King of Shaves had signed Will Carling, Will Carling would not sign a deal with a business he didn't have confidence in. Therefore the retailers felt more confident in dealing with us, that we wouldn't be going bust and they'd have to change their planogram (the way in which products are laid out on the shelf).

On 2 April 2009, a programme was broadcast on the BBC about Wellworths, a reincarnation of the Woolworths store in Dorchester. The store manager was pleasant and self-effacing and had been manager of the previous store. She not only had the guts to replace something that hadn't worked with something she thought might (same, but better) but had also got the BBC to cover it as a programme broadcast to millions and secured Chris Evans, a leading TV and radio celebrity, to open it. That's what I call leverage. Will Wellworths succeed where Woolworths failed? I hope so. It will if it stocks what customers want and need and works hard to keep its brand as an important one to the local community.

A lesson in profit

Having settled into our new office at Stone House, Herbie set about putting in place better systems. He rapidly identified that we weren't making anywhere near as much profit as we should be on the sales of our shaving oil. The company who were producing it for us seemed to be charging a lot of money and because I'd changed the artwork to incorporate Will Carling's involvement we had more origination costs.

It was at this time I learnt an important lesson from Herbie. However good your product is you must have a clear idea of the cost of producing it, selling it and what your return is. We were selling the shaving oil for £1.27 (the retailer took a standard 50 per cent margin after VAT had been deducted), but we were making the product for about £0.97, leaving just £0.30. We were selling on average 600 bottles a week, making just £180 profit before all other costs. I'm sure you can see this wasn't exactly a profitable business.

'Will, we need to sort this out, quick,' Herbie said. 'Can you do me a simple three-year business plan for King of Shaves that shows us when we're going to get near to £1 million in sales? We'll need to show something to the bank [we banked with Barclays in King Street, London] and we've got our AGM coming up, where the shareholders will need an update.'

I did the plan and what it showed was that if all the other retailers that we were targeting came on board (in addition to Boots, Tesco and Superdrug), we'd get to £1 million in sales by the year 2000. This was way too late in my opinion – seven years to hit £1 million! No one would be prepared to wait that long.

I've been conned

While our sales had been steadily growing, the chap I'd met over lunch back in January who was interested in distributing King of Shaves internationally (see page 182) had promised to arrange some meetings to present the product to potential overseas partners. I'd met him once or twice more in London, mainly at the newly opened fifth-floor restaurant at Harvey Nichols. I'd written to the people he'd suggested and heard nothing back, but he was of the view that if we could give him the distribution rights (alarm bells should have been ringing here, but weren't) then he would be able to make things happen faster.

Then he came out with a bit of a strange request. 'Will, can you lend me some money? It's just to cover some out-of-pocket expenses, you know I wouldn't normally ask but ...' Clearly I should have run a mile, but for some reason I took out my cheque book (already on its overdraft limit) and wrote him a cheque for £500 or so. Why? Don't ask me, it was a bit surreal and I didn't tell anyone about it as I guess I knew deep down something wasn't right. A couple of weeks later we met again in London to see if any of his contacts had anything. Of course they didn't and again, he asked me for some money. I said no and his attitude towards me changed. 'I'm working hard to develop your business,' he said angrily, 'and you won't pay me a few expenses. You'll be hearing from me.' And he left. The fact our sales were low, we had substantial debts and he had clearly done nothing to help us sell King of Shaves drove me to tell Ann and Herbie about it.

Herbie, who is an honest, straightforward chap said, 'I was wondering when this would happen. It always seemed strange to me that he was willing to help you, but seemed to have you doing all the work. Why did you pay him that money?'

'I don't know,' I said, 'I guess I felt indebted to him [What?] and just did.'

'Right, that's enough,' said Herbie, 'if he gets in contact with you again, tell me.'

When you are starting up a business you often find yourself grabbing at straws in the vain hope that one will have something worthwhile attached to it. I'd also been writing to other potential distributor companies, one of them being a major brand distributor called Food Brokers based in Portsmouth, and was always seeking out new ways to sell King of Shaves. Then out of the blue I received a letter from Hamish Gibson, the managing director of Food Brokers, wanting to see Herbie and me as they thought our shaving oil looked interesting.

In the same week I received a threatening letter from my conman friend: 'You've agreed to give us the rights to sell King of Shaves internationally, and if you don't honour this agreement we will sue you,' was the thrust of it. Now, I am no fool, so I knew this was complete bullshit. This letter simply reinforced what Herbie already knew, that the guy was a conman and there was only one way to deal with him. 'Leave it with me,' Herbie said. 'My brother-in-law is a solicitor, we'll set him on this crook.'

So, a letter winged its way to the 'home' address of the guy, who was based in an apartment block in Kensington, which laid out our view in no uncertain terms. We never heard from him again.

At least not until five or six years later, when Herbie, a top Belfast hairstylist called Jason Shankey and I were having lunch in a London restaurant called Hush. By this time KMI was doing well, sales were over £3 million and we were chatting to Jason about possibly developing a hairstyling line for him.

My heart stopped. At the bar, leaning in conspiratorially to another youngish guy, was my conman. Herbie realized something was up with me and followed my gaze. 'Who are you looking at? That old chap at the bar?' he quizzed.

'Yes. It's that guy who tried to con us and cost me five hundred pounds.' I stood up.

'Be careful Will,' Herbie said.

I strode over to the bar, tapped him on the shoulder and in an overloud voice spoke to the guy who he was in conversation with. 'This man is a crook and a conman. I hope you're not discussing any business with him because he'll try and do you over and if he wasn't so old, I'd punch his f***ing lights out.' It was apt that the restaurant was called Hush, as a bit of one enveloped the bar area. The conman faced me, and said nothing. 'If you ever try anything like that with me again, you'll f***ing regret it,' I said. His face turned red. I turned away, heart thumping, and returned to sit with Herbie and Jason. 'What was all that about?' Jason asked.

'Nothing. Let's go.'

Hopes dashed

Our first annual general meeting (AGM) was held at the White Hart pub in Chalfont St Giles, in a cordoned off part of the downstairs bar. I can't remember who came along; I'm pretty sure my dad did, I think Pat did and of course Herbie, Ann and me. I think they were (probably) impressed that we'd gone from £300 to £58,000 in sales, but no one was likely to make a substantial capital gain any time soon.

However, I had one trump card to play. 'Food Brokers want to meet us to discuss representing King of Shaves in a big way,' I said. 'Herbie and I are due to meet them in July and, according to their managing director, they love the product and feel it's got some really good opportunities. We'll sell to them, they'll market it and handle distribution. They're a really big company.'

'Let's hope something comes of it,' said my dad, ever encouraging.

Since Herbie had joined in April and I'd done my bit of business planning, things were starting to move inexorably upwards. Tesco had come on board with 300 stores and taken the new Will Carling pack (I don't think it sold especially well in Wales or Scotland). Sainsbury's were finally coming on board, as were Waitrose. Brian MacLaurin's firm were continually coming up with great publicity for us, England had done well in the Rugby World Cup and we were settled in our little office in Chalfont St Giles.

Emma, the young woman who had answered the telephone for me while at Chiltern House had joined. I asked her to set her own salary (à la Ricardo Semler), which her father, a senior executive at a big restaurant chain, had quizzed me about. 'It sounds like you might be taking advantage . . .' But in my eyes Emma was more than capable of setting herself a salary (which she did) and earning it. It wasn't £50,000 but nor was it £5,000. I liked the fact we'd hired her this way and in the early days this was the basis of recruitment for other employees.

I'd also taken the decision to have my crooked teeth sorted out – you'll recall Brian's comment earlier. When I was young I had a tendency to suck my thumb and over the years my front teeth had crossed slightly, which gave me a bit of a wonky smile. I was also grinding them at night due to stress, which wasn't a good thing, so in February 1995 I'd taken the decision to do something about the situation. This required two molars to be removed from my upper palate and a steel brace fitted. I'm pleased I did it as I was a bit self-conscious about my teeth and I guess I owe thanks to Brian for encouraging me to get them sorted.

When I wasn't in the dentist's chair I'd been fleshing out my three-year profit and loss statement into a more meaningful business plan. I had also come across a well-disguised loan backed by the DTI called the Loan Guarantee Scheme. The basis of the scheme was that if you had no assets (with my flat in negative equity by £25,000 this was certainly the case) then a bank would consider a loan of up to £250,000, with 85 per cent of it guaranteed by the government.

We were able to secure a loan of £100,000. This covered the trading loss to date and left a balance of £20,000 or so, which we chose to spend on paying ourselves a tiny salary and I bought a secondhand Range Rover to ferry stuff around in – dogs, clothing for Body Glove, packaging, etc. I quickly got some stickers made for the car doors that said 'Kick the Day into Play with King of Shaves'. I thought they looked cool.

Herbie and I had already had one meeting at Food Brokers, where we'd presented King of Shaves and met the board, including the founder (now sadly deceased), a chap called

Desmond Cracknell. He was certainly a larger than life character and although he appeared quite temperamental he seemed to take to Herbie and me. Things were looking good. 'We'll be in touch in a few weeks,' Hamish said. 'We think the brand has huge potential and we just need to have a final board meeting about it. It should be a formality.'

Herbie and I looked at each other and, in the naïve, starstruck way of those new in business, thought, 'That's it then. They'll sell hundreds of thousands and we'll be millionaires.' Flushed with success, I telephoned the manufacturer of our shaving oil and arranged to meet them with Herbie the following week to discuss the increase in our orders and to find out why the cost of the oil seemed high.

A couple of weeks later as we pulled into the manufacturer's car park, my mobile rang. 'Will, it's Hamish. I've got some bad news. We're not going to be pursuing the opportunity with King of Shaves.'

I was stunned. 'What?' I said, hardly able to believe what I was hearing. 'Why?'

'Desmond has decided the brand has no future and has vetoed the board's proposal to develop the range. I'm sorry.'

'I don't believe it, can't you do anything?'

'No Will, the decision's final. Why don't you call me tomorrow? There is someone I know who might be interested in handling King of Shaves. I'm sorry Will, the board and I like you and Herbie, what you've done and your vision, but it's Desmond's company.'

I hung up. 'What was that about?' asked Herbie. I didn't say anything. I threw away angrily the bottle of Ribena I'd been drinking (it hit my car and spattered it with red sticky juice). 'They don't want to do King of Shaves,' I said. 'I don't believe it.' After calming down, we went ahead with the meeting with our manufacturing partner and found out that if we could get our quantities up then cost of goods savings should be achievable.

I drove us back in silence, fuming. 'Bad decision, Desmond,' I thought, 'bad decision.' I wrote him a letter the following day (I'm never one to give up, remember!) asking what would change his mind? He wrote back, 'Nothing can change my mind Mr King. I don't see a future for your brand.'

And so our dream of having a major UK distributor working with us was over. Hamish stuck to his word and introduced us to another contact, a chap called Edwin Bessant, who'd just set up a new company called Ceuta Healthcare (now successful in its own right). We arranged to meet him. But I was deflated. Temporarily.

Out of adversity the tough get going and I simply did just that. I knew King of Shaves was starting to sell regularly and in increasingly large numbers. I knew I enjoyed shaving with it. I'd single-handedly got it stocked in Harrods, Bentalls, Boots, Superdrug, Tesco, Sainsbury's and Waitrose. It had some good publicity behind it, we'd raised £100,000 to offset the losses, Herbie and I worked well as a team (he dealt with the financial and manufacturing detail that had previously been over-whelming me) and I sensed that losing Food Brokers was a blessing in disguise. We were still in control of our own destiny and increasing numbers of consumers were shaving with King of Shaves daily. 'Shaving, lucky it's a growth business,' I thought to myself.

Gone, but not forgotten

During this time one of the shareholders in Core Brands, Tim McDowall, was murdered while on a diving holiday in Cancun,

Mexico. I heard about this when my brother, Doug, telephoned me having seen a report of it in *The Times*. I shared the same birthday as Tim, 18 August, and had met members of his family on that date in 1995. It didn't feel right continuing with Body Glove, which was struggling anyway, and at the end of 1995/early 1996 the business was formally wound up.

Chapter 12:
Turning the
Corner

Andy Hill, the chap who'd rented me the snowboard in Val d'Isère, had kept in touch and we offered him a position working alongside Julian at $uss'd, selling off the remaining stock. He proved himself to be a diligent, trustworthy and hard-working chap and quickly won the respect of myself and Herbie. After helping wind down the Body Glove business, I found Andy a role within KMI, first in a sales capacity and then in customer care. Andy writes:

As I was nearing the end of the ski season, with my twenty-seventh birthday looming on the horizon, I decided that great as life was living for six months at a time in a ski resort, I needed a new challenge in the 'real' world.

So I wrote to Will and told him why he needed a guy like me working for him — someone he can trust to get things done for him, so he can concentrate on bigger and better ideas — well that's the theory. It appeared Will agreed, although I think this was much more due to the way I'd approached him, rather than any skill set he perceived I might have.

Unfortunately the role Will had for me wasn't exactly what I had in mind (essentially working in a shop selling the clothing samples from the Body Glove range as he looked to wind down that business), but I

felt there was something in Will that was going to make the time spent in a shop worthwhile in the longer run.

So a few months later Will offered me a role in KMI working on the King of Shaves brand. I was an early convert to King of Shaves because it worked, and solved a razor burn problem for me that I knew others had too. So despite needing to bring in my own computer (an old Apple Mac my dad had got from his work for me), along with my own office chair (thanks again to my dad), a piece of plywood to act as a desk and a very small wage (£750 a month), it seemed an excellent opportunity that I wasn't going to miss. Will did also sweeten the deal with a hundred pounds towards a suit (first I'd ever owned) and a monthly diesel allowance for my (rather old and tired) little white van.

The right distributor, at long last

Sales were continuing to climb. Following the Food Brokers disappointment we had briefly worked with a third-party distributor, but had not enjoyed much success. As Herbie and I were fully immersed in keeping the business afloat, we'd asked Andy to accompany some of their sales guys on their visits to potential retailers. He was not at all impressed with them and we decided they were a waste of our money. Once again, we were back entirely on our own.

Then, while having a walk around Chalfont St Giles one lunchtime, Herbie and I went into a chemist. We always looked to see what new product was out and saw a new addition to the designer haircare shelf – a brand called Nicky Clarke. We'd heard of Nicky, he was a famous designer hairdresser based in Mayfair but we'd not seen any TV or press advertising for the brand and wondered how this chemist had come to stock it. I turned over the pack to see where the company was based and saw a label that read 'Distributed by The Sales Company', followed by a telephone number. Intrigued, I copied down the number and rang them that afternoon.

A woman called Penny Anderson answered the phone. It turned out she was a partner in the company with a guy called John Dennis. The business was based out of Penny's home in Hertfordshire, so Herbie and I arranged to visit them.

Although the Range Rover broke down en route, we made the meeting on time and were pleasantly surprised by them. Down to earth and clearly passionate about what they were doing, they were looking for more brands to handle and Penny had a strong background in product having been with Revlon. John was the salesman and Penny dealt with the operational side of the business. They were like us, a couple of hard-working businesspeople. 'Third time lucky,' I thought, as we perused their contract. They were to be paid a small monthly retainer, about £1,000 if I recall, and a percentage of sales. 'Looks alright to me,' said Herbie. 'We'll get back to you.'

Signing up The Sales Company as our distributor was one of our smartest moves. Penny and John were highly regarded by retailers, who liked what they did and how they did it. Soon joined by Jo Sigsworth (now Jo Sinclair), this great sales trio meant I didn't have to repeatedly telephone the buyers as Jo or Penny were often in with them already working on the Nicky Clarke brand or The Sanctuary (since sold to PZ Cussons for £70 million plus!). Jo Sinclair, who was pivotal to the early success of King of Shaves, actually went on to create Floraroma Ltd, her own version of KMI, out of The Brand Architekts (a company name I'd come up with for her), which we purchased from her and her business partner Michelle Doolan in 2008.

Shave.com

As well as hiring The Sales Company, another equally inspired decision was to buy the domain name, shave.com. It cost us just $35 in July 1995. I'd been watching increasing numbers of TV adverts that carried a uniform resource locator (URL) or domain name at the end. I bank with First Direct and I definitely recall http://www.firstdirect.co.uk being shown.

Intrigued by this, I started to learn as much as possible about domain names and came across a company called MarketingNet, run by Pauline and Matthew Bickerton. They'd recently made headlines as they'd painted some cows purple, which grazed by the side of the newly opened M40, which caused quite a lot of media comment.

We met with them. Their agency helped companies like ours understand the internet (not many people did back in 1995, let me assure you) and how to leverage it. 'You can use it to explain your company and products to a worldwide audience. You can provide consumers with hints and tips and in time you'll be able to sell from it!' They also suggested that we upload a picture of Will Carling and make it available for download as part of a competition. We did this via MacLaurin Communications. 'What domain do you own?' they asked. We didn't own one. I asked what would be a good one and Pauline said, 'Shave or shaving dot com, something like that, but I guess they're gone by now.'

So that evening in July 1995 I was stood outside a pub in

Chalfont St Giles waiting for the answer phone to be switched off at INTERNIC, the domain registry based in California. You couldn't e-mail them and request a domain name then or use an online agency. You had to telephone them, ask for the domain name you were interested in (shave.com I thought would be fantastic) and then pay for it by credit card. So I did just that. The next day I rang Pauline and said, 'We own shave dot com, please can you build us a site?'

To this day, this is probably one of the best business investments we've ever made. The shave.com site has had hundreds of millions of visitors, is often the biggest shaving brand website world-wide in terms of traffic numbers and since we've had it, and other domains like kingofshaves.com and kingofshaves.co.uk, it is deeply embedded in search engines like Google, to the extent that if you type in 'shave', King of Shaves is the top find, with no search engine optimization needed.

As important as the internet was in 1995, it is even more important today. It's a vital business tool to promote and leverage your company or brand. You are able to stay in touch with consumers world-wide and use the power of blogs and social-networking sites and services like Twitter to keep people up to speed with your business news, hopes, aspirations and general commentary. I embrace the web wholeheartedly.

Strategic development of the business

The internet, the growth of men's magazines, such as *FHM*, *Loaded* and *Maxim*, in the mid-1990s and the 'Beckham effect' were three key drivers in accelerating awareness and sales of men's grooming products. Understanding these factors and exploiting them where possible definitely helped keep King of

Shaves ahead of the game. At this time, our only competitors in men's shaving brands were Gillette, Wilkinson Sword and Colgate Palmolive. There weren't any of the metrosexual, niche, high-end brands that have sprung up over the past decade. We were in the vanguard of men's grooming and although we didn't really know it, we were starting to build a strong brand momentum in users and sales.

With The Sales Company on board and working well and agencies working for us on web, publicity and sales promotion, we found that we had much more time to think strategically about developing the business. 'What about developing another product?' I said to Herbie one day. 'Another shaving oil maybe, with some different ingredients, I think aloe and vitamin E are good for the skin and I've heard quite a bit about AHAs [alpha hydroxy acids].' Why it had taken us over two years to consider adding another product to the one we already had, I have no idea. Now, we launch ranges of products to different retailers all the time. Maybe it was a confidence thing. I guess we were nervous about the sales of our original oil and that creating a new product might have been a little premature.

In February 1996 we introduced Formula Alpha alongside our Original Formula shaving oil and, even better, had managed to secure a promotional space with Boots at a cost of £18,000 for four weeks. The order that was placed for the promotion was substantial and our sales jumped in that period.

At the same time, we also modified the packaging, from a bottle held to a card by a plastic blister to the same bottle held within a polypropylene tube so it looked a little like a can. The packaging was pretty unique and I think we might have won an award for it.

King of Shaves down under

In early 1996 I received a phone call from an enthusiastic British guy who lived in New Zealand. His name is Dave McLeod, and he and his friend and business partner, Paul Irwin, demonstrate exactly what is needed to start a business from scratch, keep the faith, and ultimately reap the rewards. Here is a quick summary of their experience down under with King of Shaves:

Our experience with KMI began in 1996. Our company, Creative Partners Limited (CPL), began in somewhat unusual circumstances. A mutual friend introduced us to King of Shaves shaving oil. Little did we know that this would be a start of a very special business arrangement.

We made a call to Will in the UK and explained that we were interested in becoming the Australasian distributors for the brand. We also used poetic licence when it came to our existing business exploits, telling him that we imported and distributed products from the UK when in fact CPL had yet to be formed. Will was very open to a conversation about supplying stores on the other side of the planet. Convinced we would be millionaires overnight, CPL launched King of Shaves shaving oil in New Zealand. Utilizing the assistance of a group of beautiful girls (later named the Shave Squad) we booked the centre court areas in four of the largest shopping malls in Auckland and had the girls shave potential customers.

Open sharing of marketing ideas has been a big part of the KMI/CPL relationship. KMI used the face of Will Carling to stimulate sales, so adopting this idea CPL presented our case to the All Blacks' captain Sean Fitzpatrick. Unfortunately we were unable to come to mutually beneficial agreement (for some reason Sean wanted to be paid for us to profit from the use of his image!). Several years later, the Shave Squad idea was adopted by KMI in the UK.

Over the years KMI's new product development and new brands have been hard to keep up with. In true business entrepreneurial style it seems like virtually every month a change of design or something revolutionary has been added to the KMI portfolio. When it comes to product development KMI has a very unconventional way of looking at things. Not much had changed in the soaps and shower gels category until Will and his team had a look at it, then what seemed like overnight a line extension to the King of Shaves body sprays appeared and air-powered foaming body washes. It stood out on the shelf, which in a world of 'me too' products and brands means an awful lot.

In 2002 we got the call from Will explaining that they had just signed a licensing agreement with a brand that could have a huge potential impact on the Australian side of our business. The product range they had developed was a range of chlorine-clearing shampoos and conditioners (ideal for swimmers) and the brand they were working with was the Aussie icon Speedo. Hydrocreatine was the new buzzword for the product range – KMI had developed a way for the supplement creatine to be easily absorbed into the skin. CPL pitched the brand to the Australian supermarkets and pharmacies and received impressive buy-in.

Rightly or wrongly, cost of goods has little or no consequence to Will and his team when creating new products. High-quality ingredients, distinctive packaging and speed to market are all that really seem to matter and from a distributor point of view this can be a bittersweet experience. Over the years there have been several products in the KMI portfolio that are attractive from a consumer point of view but prohibitive in price. The flip side of this is that we can say with all confidence that the quality of the products we supply is high and ultimately they do what they say they will do.

Open and honest communication and support was always forthcoming from Will and his team and after a major review of our margins and profitability, Will could see that we would need a significantly better pricing model as well as improved trading terms for us to succeed. Will was instrumental in making these changes, as well as helping us set up operations in Sydney, Australia, which was the start of the next evolution in our business. After nearly six years of struggle we could clearly see the way forward and *after the initial learning experiences, our Australian business has taken off.*

Will has an infectious 'can do' attitude that is shared among the whole team at KMI and once again it's something that has been adopted by us at CPL. He has been successful and he wants you to be successful too. In markets such as New Zealand and Australia, diversification is the key to growth. Will has introduced us to other companies looking to expand globally and I believe he takes great pride in watching us grow.

For almost eight years there has been talk of King of Shaves moving into the hardware (razor) side of the market, a category that is at least five times the size of the software (shave prep) category. So when KMI announced in June 2008 that they were finally launching the new Azor we were ecstatic.

Here in New Zealand, CPL launched the Azor in November 2008. We relaunched the Shave Squad and put them in a Hummer H3, sending them out to the streets to spread the word and shave New Zealand men. Even celebrities such as David Beckham and Jeremy Clarkson got pictured with the team!

To sum up, working with Will and the KMI team is like working with extended family. From day one it has never been the usual supplier/distributor arrangement. Ideas and visions are shared, hospitality enjoyed and we believe that as the future unfolds and as both our companies continue to flourish, so will our relationship.

Reading these words from Dave and Paul means a huge amount to me. They've had to trust us, 12,000 miles away, that we have a business that can supply them with the world's best toiletries products. Conversely, we've trusted that they had the enthusiasm, skills and persistence to make KMI a success in their markets. The Azor is doing extremely well in New Zealand, with over 15 per cent market share for the handle and is destined to launch in Australia in early 2010, so watch this space!

Things weren't always this encouraging in the Australian market though. For example, having only recently registered King of Shaves in the UK, and before we met Dave and Paul, a friend of Ann's said she had heard a King of Shaves shaving oil being advertised in Australia while she was recently there on holiday. 'We don't sell in Australia,' I said to Ann, 'she must be mistaken.'

She wasn't. We managed to find out that a shaving oil called King of Shaves was being promoted on the radio in Sydney and through some contacts (I forget who) we managed to get a sample. It was exactly like our bottle, even down to the crown. We don't own a monopoly on shaving oil, but you'd think they'd have called it something different. I met with Marks & Clerk to show them the pack and they said they'd get hold of their associate firm in Australia to see whether that company had attempted to register for a trademark in Australia. 'What if they have?' I said.

'Then you've got a problem, you won't be able to sell your product there,' was the daunting reply.

I was not having that and proceeded to tell Katherine what I thought about it.

'Well, let's see,' she said. 'Leave it with us.'

The matter was resolved in our favour but at a cost to us of about £5,000.

Balls in the air

As you read this book, I hope you see how many balls you have to keep in the air to ensure your business doesn't fall over and go bust. When you are starting up, you are so vulnerable to every little thing. For example, a retailer not settling an account on time, which means you can't pay your bills, which might mean a court bailiff coming round to see which of your assets he might take (yes, this happened to us). You *have* to keep on top of your accounts. With our company having made losses for years, we were consistently claiming VAT back. I once spent a particularly gruelling five hours with a VAT inspector, when I thought I was on top of everything, only to have my (independently prepared) VAT returns reassessed to discover we owed a few thousand pounds in unpaid VAT. I still shudder thinking about it. There was no deception but where the VAT is concerned you are guilty until the inspector walks away having pronounced you innocent!

There are many more examples of the multitude of tasks that needed to be done. Luckily, Emma and Andy were great workers. Emma dealt with the accounting and finance and Andy started to develop into a production management role, with his engineering degree standing him in good stead from an analytical perspective, combined with his ability to apply common sense to any issue.

Product development overdrive

Having launched a second oil, we talked with Penny, John and Jo, our sales development manager, about further new products. 'Why not do a shaving gel?' they said.

'I don't want to do a canned gel,' I retorted, 'they're rubbish, that's why we did an oil.'

'Isn't there something you can develop then?' they asked.

Herbie and I looked at each other. I guessed we could do a gel containing aloe and put it in a recyclable tube, but wondered how we could get the oil into it. I was insistent it somehow had the benefits of oil to aid the shave, but being water-based, and oil and water not mixing, this was a problem. 'I've seen a bath product with little microcapsules in it,' said Herbie unexpectedly. 'Maybe we could put the oil inside the microcapsules?'

'Yes,' I thought, immediately trying to think of a name for it. 'We could call it . . . an AlphaGel, an AlphaGel DDS shaving gel.

'What's DDS?' he asked.

'Dual Delivery System,' I said.

'It sounds cool.'

And so two new products were born: our award-winning AlphaGels, Natural Unmentholated and Supercooled Menthol.

Jo called us on the way back from Boots, having presented prototypes of the gels. 'They'll take them,' she said, 'in July. But they thought you were going to do men's skincare as well?' Herbie and I looked at each other. Just a few weeks ago we had one oil. Now we had two oils and two gels and the buyer wanted more. 'How many do you think they'd take?' I asked.

'Four – a face wash, a face scrub, an aftershave gel and a moisturizer,' she answered. 'Can you get something mocked up?'

It was at about this time that I was first introduced to Simon Watson, now our head of design, by Andy. Simon was working for an advertising agency, Ambleglow. His recollections help me remember what it was like back then:

In 1996 I was working for a small design and advertising agency in Maidenhead. I had spent six years earning my spurs in central London cutting my teeth on high-end corporate design projects and now I was working on everything from conservatory leaflets (Lord forgive me for I have graphically sinned) to recruitment advertising campaigns for the local borough council. When an old school friend, Andy Hill, called up asking for some help with a leaflet for a shaving oil, I just added it to the eclectic mix of work that was on my plate.

That first year we did three jobs for King of Shaves. I met Will and Herbie in KMI's small offices in Chalfont St Giles. They were chain-smoking Marlboro Reds and two dogs were adding to the aroma. It was a baptism of fire – Will's seemingly random thoughts and comments being machine-gunned at me, Herbie viewing me suspiciously (who trusts someone in advertising anyway?) and I remember getting back into my car, wondering how I was ever going to please them, let alone meet their brief (if you could call it that).

I learned the hard way. The briefs from Will were always, at best, pretty fluid. The distrust of designers and advertising executives was very evident and my ego got a severe pasting. But eventually I think I won them over. Will started coming over to our offices in Maidenhead to sit with me so he could 'brain dump' his thoughts on to the screen via my mouse. It was horribly frustrating at times and after two or three hours sitting with Will I was left mentally exhausted. On the printer would be the result of this 'workout' and often it was something that would have got me banged-up for life for crimes against design.

The challenge for me would be to turn these streams of consciousness into something that would excite Will and satisfy my creative nature. Sometimes that would happen and I would go home knowing my design would be in shops, being purchased by thousands of people. I would feel absolutely on top of the world. But when I could not change Will's mind, when he had a vision that looked awful to me and insisted on it, those days I would just take the money and go home.

But I must have been doing something right. After three years we were working on over a hundred projects a year for KMI, some of them substantial pieces of business, including national advertising campaigns. Will could (and can be) pretty random at times. Yet when it came, the job offer was surprising, though it was delivered in typical Will King fashion, at an FHM grooming awards ceremony, and it was sealed (on a napkin if memory serves) with Will and Herbie in a pub in Chesham. So I joined KMI in 2001, with my gorgeous Apple Mac, printer and scanner among several beige PCs, plus Will's two (smelly) dogs living under my table.

Eight years on I have watched the company grow

> *and while I think Will has mellowed just a bit, he can still be very manic, very driven and full of ideas – some mad as a March hare, others bordering on genius. I am lucky enough to be involved in a company where change is embraced and nothing is taken for granted. And I can thank Will for that.*

As well as getting good product design, we needed a reputable, reliable and innovative manufacturer for our new products. Through Peter Wallis of OPS Management, a consultant who'd worked with us on our shaving-oil manufacture, we were introduced to a chap called Mike Peters, the owner of leading contract manufacturer Universal Products (Lytham) Manufacturing Ltd (UPL), based in Lytham, Lancashire.

Herbie and Andy drove up to meet him and he agreed to help us develop our AlphaGel and new skincare range. I'm delighted that UPL and Mike continue to be one of our key partners today, fourteen years on, always willing to go the extra mile to help us develop new products and ideas, even if they never hit the shelves or sell what we expect of them.

Year three comes to a close
Let's take a look at how the profit and loss statement for King of Shaves had changed over the first three years of trading:

Year 1
£300 in sales
£30,000 in losses – shareholder- and personal debt-financed

Year 2
£58,000 in sales

£70,000 in losses – partially financed by £100,000 from the DTI Loan Guarantee Scheme

Year 3
£250,000 in sales

£20,000 in losses – financed by increase in overdraft facility, increase in DTI loan and by assigning our invoices to Alex Lawrie (the UK's largest factoring company) for payment

Total losses: £120,000 over three years

Chance of being backed by a Dragon from the Den? Zero. What would the next year bring?

We were getting consistently good write-ups in the media for our products, had launched the new skincare range, K-Series, with Boots and our AlphaGels were starting to sell a few thousand a month, then over the course of the year, tens, then hundreds of thousands. As we weren't able to spend any money on advertising, this growth could only be down to publicity and word-of-mouth recommendation. It was clear that people were enjoying shaving with King of Shaves as much as I was and I dreamt of launching a major ad campaign to really go up against our 'can-ventional' competitors. In spring 1996, aged thirty-one, I was starting to feel that we had a success on our hands.

Opportunity knocks
At about this time, Emma asked me if I'd help her dad move some office furniture to his home in my Range Rover. 'No

problem,' I thought. As I drove him to his home he asked in a casual sort of way, 'I bet when you retire it'll be in the Caribbean?'

'Well, I'm a long way off being successful enough to retire,' I answered. 'Why do you ask?'

'A friend of ours is selling some land in the Caribbean, are you interested?'

Now, most normal people with no money and a three-year-old business still not in profit would almost certainly say no. But what was the harm in learning more? I'd come to love the Caribbean, having been to Grenada with my girlfriend in April 1992 for a holiday, and thought to myself, 'If I ever do well enough to retire, it could indeed be in the West Indies, with a yacht, etc.' 'Yes, could be,' I ventured.

'I'll get her to call you then, OK?'

'OK.'

I thought nothing more of it, until one night I was in London shopping with Ann and my phone rang. 'Hello, is that William?'

'Yes.'

'I understand you want to buy my land.'

'Umm, well, maybe . . . but I don't actually know where it is!'

'Oh. Grenada. Have you heard of it?'

Silence.

'Sounds interesting, where in Grenada, exactly?'

'L'Anse aux Epines. It's on the beach.'

L'Anse aux Epines was where Ann's parents lived. 'We'll get back to you, we need to speak to some people,' I said.

'OK, well don't leave it too long.'

Amazed, I hung up. Of all the Caribbean islands it was in Grenada and of all the parts of Grenada it was in the best area, where the best hotels were, close to the airport. We called Ann's dad, explained where the property was and asked him to call back. He called back within half an hour. 'Buy it,' he said.

Easier said than done. But it seemed like a chance of a lifetime, something that we'd only consider doing if we knew it had a great recommendation; after all, buying an acre and a half of land, sight unseen, in the West Indies isn't something you do every day. So I set to raising the deposit money for a mortgage (Ann's dad said he might be able to help us arrange a mortgage in Grenada) but we needed £30,000 as the seller wanted £100,000 for it (it's now worth about $2 million). My mum and dad chipped in, I borrowed some money via another loan and Ann cashed in some of her savings. But we were still way short by some margin and I couldn't see any way of getting the balance together.

I've always thought laterally. The important thing was to get the land and worry about the 'how's it going to be sorted out?' later. So I telephoned Pat, one of the founding King of Shaves shareholders and asked him if he fancied involvement in a bit of land in the Caribbean. Ann and I were getting married in Grenada the following year, so Pat knew I was serious and asked 'How much and when?' He came in on the deal and we got the land. The transaction completed the day before our marriage in February 1997 and there's now a beautiful villa, Kingfisher, nestling on it. Opportunity knocked and we took it.

Never knock opportunity – here's why. *The New York Times'* bestseller *The Black Swan*, by Nassim Nicholas Taleb, says this about opportunity:

Seize any opportunity, or anything that looks like opportunity. They are rare, much rarer than you think. Remember that positive Black Swans (a Black Swan is an event with rarity, extreme impact and retrospective) have a necessary first step: you need to be exposed to them. Many people do not realize that they are getting a lucky break in life when they get it. If a big publisher (or art dealer or movie executive or hotshot banker or big thinker) suggests an appointment, cancel anything that you have planned: you may never see such a window open up again. I am sometimes shocked at how little people realize that these opportunities do not grow on trees.

I couldn't agree more. After all, my creation of the King of Shaves shaving oil might be viewed as a 'Black Swan', given its unlikelihood and impact down the track on our market and competition.

Out of the valley of death

As 1996 ended it looked like our annual sales (1 January–31 December) would be about £500,000 and, shock of shocks, we might make £1,000 in profit! We'd decided to change our accounting period from ending in March to ending in December. I guess it just seemed like common sense that our financial year tied in with the year's end, and as December had always been our biggest sales month, it gave us the chance to end the year on a high.

Herbie and I had started to pay ourselves a salary, about £20,000 per year each, and it looked like sales of over £1 million could be achieved in 1997. Looking back now upon the fact that it took us five years of slog, throwing the dice and rethrowing the dice to achieve this level of sales, it is pretty amazing. Most people would have given up after year one and certainly by year three with losses running at £100,000. But I believed in King of Shaves. I genuinely believed our product was king and in years four and five we broke the back of 'the valley of death'. The valley of death is my name for the early, often loss-making years of a business, when you have to work twenty-four seven just to keep it going. More often than not it's a hand-to-mouth existence. Not quite life or death but it feels that way.

So, if you are preparing to ride into the valley of death with your own business, keep faith in yourself and your business, for it is only you who can get through to the sun on the other side, where your business has momentum, profitability and cash flow and where you can plan for the future with ever-growing confidence.

I guess 1997 was the year that I really felt we had a growing and, more importantly, profitable business on our hands. Herbie and I were gaining in confidence. We had a small, sales-focused team and the King of Shaves brand was starting to develop a strong momentum.

We looked into range extensions for King of Shaves – body-spray deodorants and air-powered shower gels under the trademark Kinetik®. Although they were ultimately unsuccessful (we simply couldn't manufacture them cost-effectively enough to hit the price points the retailers demanded), the fact we'd gone from shaving oils, to gels, to skincare and now into wash and fragrance demonstrated to us that as long as the product is great, anything is possible.

I married Ann in February 1997 in a happy ceremony at Fort Frederick, a hilltop fort overlooking the Grenadian capital of St George's. We'd been able to travel there knowing that King of Shaves was being looked after by Andy and Emma back home. They sent a funny telegram that said:

Congratulations on your marriage, Stop. All fine back home, Stop. Have sold the company, Stop. Cheque in the post, Stop. Best wishes, Emma and Andy.

And things got better. I was driving to work and was listening to David 'Kid' Jensen on the radio. He mentioned a phrase that stuck in my mind, about living life 'twenty-four seven'. I thought it was a neat phrase and as soon as I got into work I applied for a trademark for 24SEVEN and set to work creating a range of body-spray deodorants that might compete with Lynx.

More employees had joined us. Jane Greenaway has this to say of her experience with KMI in the early days:

I find it incredible to believe that I've spent the past eleven years working for KMI. Employed as a production controller, I joined the company when there were only four other people: Will, Herbie, Andy and Katie, the office administrator.

In those days we had only eight King of Shaves products and a comparable number of customers and suppliers. I'd been working in a similar role for a very successful greetings-card company in London. Tired of the commute, I replied to an advertisement in our local paper. Details were sketchy but what was there matched my experience.

I remember the interviews vividly. I liked the fact that Will reflected a typical entrepreneur, full of enthusiasm and creative ideas. Herbie seemed much tougher, a numbers man with huge attention to detail. This was a very similar combination to the partners of my previous company, which had proved to be so successful. Andy appeared very hands-on, he's known as the 'Discovery Channel' as he just knows about everything and to this day, is still the person I would choose as my 'phone a friend' if I ever went for the million.

The fourth member of the interview panel was a bit more of a surprise, especially as our first meeting was him sniffing my knees during the interview! A wire-haired fox terrier named Dudley, Will's pride and joy and I quickly realized, an integral part of the team.

KMI agreed to match my London salary, but I found it more than a little surreal in those early days. I'd been used to a highly pressured environment as a buyer with lead times of days and the support of a business system. Suddenly I found myself back in the world of Excel spreadsheets with three-month lead times. I soon discovered I was to become a master of all trades, as is necessary in such a small business. If Will had to attend meetings away from the office, I'd be asked to take Dudley for a walk in the beautiful surrounding countryside.

There were also worrying times in those early days; had I made the right decision? I heard rumours of large loans, bailiffs and the payment of employees with personal cheques. Apparently I was lucky to have a chair when I arrived as Andy had had to provide his own!

Getting into fashion brands

In June 1997 Herbie and I were chatting in the office and he said he'd been looking at fashion brands that might consider licensing a company like us to produce a fragrance for them. Calvin Klein had launched cK1 and Tommy Hilfiger, Tommy, and he thought we could do the same. Talk about increasing belief in our abilities! Top of his list were Ted Baker and Paul Smith. He put in a call to the latter, but we heard nothing back, whereas we managed to secure a meeting with Ray Kelvin, the founder of Ted Baker, having spoken to one of his colleagues. Ted Baker were just about to float, with sales of £14 million, and had made a name for themselves by producing beautifully detailed shirts, always with a unique personality. In fact, they regarded themselves as 'fashion's best kept secret'.

In July we turned up at their office (called The Fortress, the previous one had been called The Bunker) and were shown into a meeting room. The office was a hive of activity; they were floating on the stock market literally the next day and suits from Goldman Sachs were running around, huddling in meetings and making calls. It was very exciting.

We sat there for quite a while and thought about what we were going to say, given that our experience of producing a fine fragrance was a big fat zero and we'd be competing with major brands like Boss, Calvin Klein, Ralph Lauren and others to secure shelf space.

Ray entered the room, followed by two or three colleagues, including his head of design, a quiet chap called Ed Potter. My recollection of the meeting is a little hazy, as there was such a big personality in the room (Ray) and we weren't exactly a multimillion pound company.

'So, what can I do for you?' Ray asked.

'We'd like to develop a fragrance for Ted Baker,' Herbie said.

'What's your experience?'

'Well, we have a brand called King of Shaves, have you heard of it?' Silence. Then someone in the room said, 'I know King of Shaves, it's a shaving oil, it's really good, do you want us to sell it from our stores?'

'No, we want to design, manufacture and market a fragrance under the Ted Baker name. We've got some really good ideas.'

There was a knock on the door, a suit poked his head in and said, 'Ray, we need to talk to you about something.' Ray left (he was floating his company after all, I think he had much bigger things than us on his mind) and was followed by his colleagues. Herbie and I looked at each other. This wasn't exactly going to plan. We sat there, thinking what to say next. Or, was that it?

We waited for about 20 minutes or so and at last the door opened and Ray returned. 'Sorry about that, big day for us. Now, tell me again, what do you want to do for Ted?' Herbie explained that we felt we had the skills, abilities and retail contacts to launch a fragrance brand under the Ted Baker name that would be a great success. 'You know Ted has a no-advertising policy?' Ray said.

'Yes,' replied Herbie. 'It's going to be a challenge, but I believe we can do something really successful for you.'

Silence. 'Well, thanks for coming in. I like what you've had to say. Can you work up some ideas for me? Liaise with Ed Potter, he handles this sort of stuff, and when you're ready, we'll see what you come up with.'

Well, you couldn't say fairer than that! Herbie and I left the building in a bit of a daze. We were obviously delighted we'd got to the next stage, but now we had to come up with something that would get Ray, and his head of design, excited.

I don't intend to go into our relationship with Ted Baker in this book other than to say it's been a really satisfying and rewarding one for us, one which neatly complements King of Shaves and one that Herbie especially is proud of. Although I was heavily involved in selecting the design of the first fragrance, Ted Baker Skinwear, the relationship with Ted Baker has very much been Herbie's. Ray and I have a strong respect for each other. I'm a massive fan of how he has cleverly built the brand since founding it in 1988 and I'm delighted he thinks our Azor is great. If King of Shaves can be a fraction as successful as Ted Baker, I'll be a happy chap.

In recounting this story about how we got involved with Ted Baker, a lot of things come back to me about the behavioural traits of Herbie and me; always being the best we can be, making the best products possible, for the best companies and customers.

Don't fear the unknown. Where the design of the fragrance for Ted Baker was concerned, clearly we didn't have the in-house capability to design it, but we knew who could be really good at it under our direction. And if you can start a business from just one 'halo' product (ours was a shaving oil, Ted Baker's was a detailed shirt) then this halo can in time hover over all manner of different products. My advice is, don't fear failure. Never knock opportunity. Take a deep breath and just do it.

Chapter 13: Breaking into the US Market

Between 1997 and late 2002 the KMI and King of Shaves business simply grew. We became increasingly confident about our ability to develop, manufacture and publicize our products. As well as King of Shaves and Ted Baker, we'd launched 24SEVEN into Boots and were selling ever-increasing amounts of product to Paul and Dave in New Zealand.

In 1997 we were telephoned by a chap called Ian Ginsberg, who owned New York's best-known pharmacy, C.O. Bigelow, in Greenwich Village. He'd bought our shaving oil on a trip to the UK and was interested in distributing it. He ran a distributor business supplying retailers like his across the US with quirky, unusual, cutting-edge products. We agreed a distribution deal with him, as he seemed honest, down to earth and likeable.

As 1997 drew to a close, we could see we were finally going to make a decent trading profit of £125,000 on sales of approx £1.25 million. At last. We'd broken the £1 million sales mark, five years after I'd started the business. Result. To celebrate, Herbie and I awarded ourselves a pay increase for the forthcoming year (about £40,000 each; I'd last earned this amount in 1991) and decided to go on a skiing trip to Val d'Isère together – great fun.

The satisfaction of success for me was obvious:

- King of Shaves starting to become a household name, with sales in excess of £2.5 million at retail (£1.25 million wholesale)
- Ted Baker Skinwear 'in development'
- I was married
- I owned 1.25 acres of beachfront land in Grenada

The following few years brought more success. As the momentum of our brands grew, so did the sales and our ability to sell them to retailers. In 1998, including the launch of Ted Baker Skinwear, sales topped £2 million. This was despite the fact that our small office was burned to the ground. The supermarket in Chalfont St Giles that we were located above caught fire and we lost everything. However, we quickly set the business up in Herbie's front room, rebuilt our database and accounts and didn't miss delivering a single order. Jane recalls:

There was always an air of anticipation. You just knew that the company was going to succeed. There was such passion and drive coming from the top. Exciting times were bound to be ahead. Things were certainly starting to change at an amazing rate. We were just about to launch the first Ted Baker range, Skinwear, which would totally change our business model.

However, just five months after I joined the company, we were hit with what could have been a massive setback. In the early hours of Father's Day 1998 the offices were burned to the ground. Unfortunately we were not as meticulous as we should have been with our back-ups and every record we had went up in flames. I believe the only thing to come out of those offices were three distorted bottles of our K-24 moisturizer, which Will still has, set in clear resin.

Rather than destroying the business, the reaction to this terrible event has been typical of my experiences in KMI — to succeed in the face of adversity. The

> *company was founded during the recession of the early 1990s and many of the company's ventures, particularly the Azor, show how the company thrives in a David and Goliath environment.*

We hired more talented employees – Lisa Coulstock to work on Ted Baker products and Karen Brookes (now Karen Heygate-Browne) to work alongside Andy in production and operations. We gradually upgraded our systems, moving from ordering products based on Andy's trusty Excel-based spreadsheets to a more sophisticated order processing system. Ken Lamacraft Marketing Ltd worked with Herbie and I, focusing on developing the Ted Baker business.

In 1999 sales nearly doubled again, to £3.9 million. And, to my delight, I became a father to Cameron Halcyon King, born 5 December 1999.

I think the years 1998 to 2000 were probably the most exciting we had, until recently when we launched the Azor. The feeling of commercial momentum building in a company is very intoxicating. As long as you keep your feet on the ground where managing the growth is concerned, then your company should succeed. Andy has this to say:

> *From 1998 onwards the company's tack changed and we moved into multiple brands, both owning and licensing brands across the health and beauty sector, using the knowledge we gained on King of Shaves and*

applying it elsewhere. As the business grew we took on more people, many of whom had no comprehension of what it was like in the early days and just saw Will and Herbie as rich and successful, not knowing or even appreciating the sacrifices they made and the gambles they took on the way up and how close at times the business had come to a big fall.

However, as any business grows the culture changes and it's hard to hold on to all the things that made us a great company in the early days as so much can get diluted down. People try and use money to replace creativity. I once heard Anita Roddick on Radio 4 saying that she was at her most creative in the early days when they had no money, because when there's no money the creativity flows, because it has to. Napoleon said, 'I don't need great generals, I need lucky ones, as lucky ones win battles.' Will always felt we were a lucky company and so far he's been right.

Some of the people we took on found Will and Herbie a challenge to work with, which is understandable as working with the two-headed dog (as I call them) is a skill that I've spent many years learning. There's a lot of detail in our business. Will doesn't really get involved in detail as he's a champion delegator, so delegates it out and leaves it to the likes of me to get it sorted.

Most people new to the business have had to have the drunken chat from Will where he asks them where they want to be in three to five years' time and how big and impressive a job title they'd like. This seems to have mixed results, from scaring people witless to giving them delusions of grandeur. Will is genuinely keen to see those he likes happy. It matters to him – almost I think it reassures him that everything is OK.

King of Shaves meets Uncle Sam

Developing scale, solid infrastructure and a talented staff, such as Andy, Karen, Jane and Lisa, meant that we could concentrate on spinning the bigger plates. Between 1995 and 1999 Herbie and I spent quite a lot of time in the USA, working out how we could build our business there. Ian (Ginsberg of C.O. Bigelow, see page 231) was doing a great job but I knew King of Shaves's future lay with major nationwide retailers there – Target, CVS/pharmacy, Walgreens and the like.

'If I can get two or three of our products into twenty thousand US stores, then we've got a really big business on our hands,' I said to myself. Having worked in the USA before doing his MBA at INSEAD, Herbie spent more time there than I did and was meeting more and more people who seemed as if they wanted to work with us. However, once we met them or saw the paperwork (onerous distribution agreements) we had second thoughts. That was until I took a call from a vice president at Target, who had seen King of Shaves on a UK visit and thought it would sell well in their 1,500 stores. I was actually in Grenada when he called – the office had given him my number there – and just like that he asked us to come to Minneapolis, meet his men's grooming team and work out a deal. Amazing!

The problem was we had absolutely no infrastructure in the

US and no money to finance our expansion there. We met with Barclays and showed them a business plan for the US with a view to borrowing more money. They said no so we then tried Lloyds TSB and met with Nigel Gibson, who agreed to provide a £500,000, four-year term loan to facilitate brand expansion for King of Shaves into the US.

Herbie had also met a well-qualified lady, ex-Wharton School of Management, who could serve as our first US CEO. We flew her into the UK, had dinner at my home and on that basis (and her CV) hired her. As it turned out, she could drive a mean spreadsheet but on the sales front was weak, so we parted company with her in November 2001.

I guess our US launch was an example of confidence over common sense rather than confidence and common sense! To launch the brand we spent $50,000 renting an apartment for the night in New York, complete with singing Elvises, products floating in black baths and an abundance of champagne. We had wildly optimistic sales numbers in our mind for the 1,500 Target stores. We hadn't really realized how absolutely enormous the US is or how difficult it is to publicize products there on a national level. Each state essentially behaves like a separate country and there were no national men's media titles we could get access to (in time we built a great relationship with *FHM*, but that closed in the US a few years ago).

We thought we'd get other retailers to list King of Shaves (it took us until 2003 to get another retailer) and we thought sales would be in the tens of thousands per week, comparable with our UK sales. In fact, we achieved a fraction of our original sales expectations. The £500,000 loan didn't last very long, what with a 'heavyweight' CEO to pay, an office to run, publicity budgets and ever-increasing expenses. We soon realized that we were going to make a substantial loss in the US in our first year, not exactly what we'd told Lloyds TSB.

Having been dragged over the coals at the bank by Nigel and warned that we might be in breach of the dreaded covenants, Herbie and I took action to stem losses in the US. With our CEO having been asked to resign, the responsibility of running the US business came to rest on a young graduate, Stephanie Eddy (hired by the CEO as her assistant).

Stephanie, aged just twenty-one when she was hired, was a stellar find. Since 2000 she's grown into a superbly capable young businesswoman who now runs our US office out of New York. She oversees sales in the millions of dollars and is respected and loved by all those who work with her. Finding people like this, who are capable of understanding a vision, who work hard to make it a reality, who are honest, trust-worthy and never afraid to speak their mind is absolutely critical if you are to scale up your business. Indeed, since 2001 much of my time has been spent looking for and hiring talented individuals who don't work in a conventional way, but just make things happen. I've asked Stephanie to describe her experience working with us – I hope you agree, it makes interesting reading!

It's been nine years since I graduated from Wesleyan University with a BA in American Studies and I'm still working for the same company I started with that summer of 2000. I'm probably not the only person from my graduating class still with their first employer, but I know I'm one of the very few. When I moved to New York City that summer I was pretty sure

I would venture into the world of PR. However, an invitation to a Shaving Elvis party led to a career with Will and King of Shaves.

The US business embarked on a series of up-and-down rides and I landed the enviable position of VP sales and operations (aka US watchdog and sole New York employee) at the age of twenty-four. I was surprised and flattered that Will and Herbie were comfortable with this arrangement.

Over the next few years Will spent a great deal of time in the US. I tagged along to his meetings and learned about negotiating and selling. He made it clear that I was responsible for handling the US office and his encouragement raised my confidence in myself. In reality, he was making the engine run in the US but people working with us certainly respected me more than they otherwise would have because of the manner in which Will presented me.

In one of Will's many linguistic twists, he branded me a 'scepthiast' because I was pretty much always enthusiastic, yet sceptical. I'd have to agree with that assessment. In 2003 I gave my first presentation at a sales conference. While I didn't close any deals, I would have stayed in the wings if Will hadn't encouraged me to start interacting with buyers on a higher level. I was nervous, yet thrilled to be speaking for the brand on my own. The rest of that week was a blur of King of Shaves introductions and we were both exhausted at the end. So Will suggested what any boss

238

and his employee would do after days of meetings in Florida. 'Why don't we go to SeaWorld for a few hours?' And we did.

Many people wonder how King of Shaves has come so far. Will's leadership is obviously the catalyst. We are vastly outgunned by our competition in marketing dollars, but Will is open to any idea that will help the US business turn the next corner. Many marketers would love to work with King of Shaves to help us overcome our biggest competitor – lack of awareness. It's tempting to try to throw every dollar we have at the challenge and we receive countless pitches asking about our marketing budget. One of Will's best lines is, 'I'm not going to give you a budget, or you're just going to spend it.' He challenges us to use our brains and tell him what we really need to achieve any given task.

It would be difficult to understate the ups and downs that the US office has had. We've been in situations where we were signing Jason Kidd, a major NBA star, for a two-year King of Shaves endorsement and immediately three new major US retailers were stocking King of Shaves. Turn the corner and we've hit some major challenges. But along the way there have been a few constants. Primarily it has been Will's confidence that King of Shaves is becoming a major global brand.

Fish and Speedo

In 2001 opportunity knocked again in the form of Paul Burfoot, owner of the Fish hairstyling salon based in D'Arblay Street, Soho. He was looking for a partner to help him launch a range of Fish 'Born in Soho' styling products. He'd come up with a great word – Unisexy® – which I liked. Working with Jo (now running her own business, The Brand Architekts), we launched Fish in Boots and have never looked back. The range now sells millions of pounds worth of Fish Fingers, Stone Fish and Angel Fish products each year.

Our confidence was growing and as we approached ten years in business we made a decision to spin just one more plate. It was a decision that nearly derailed the company, but it made me concentrate even more on our core business, King of Shaves.

Through Ray at Ted Baker we were introduced to Pentland Group, a hugely successful owner of sports and fashion brands, probably best known for building then selling Reebok for hundreds of millions of pounds. Their portfolio of brands included Berghaus, Mitre, Red or Dead, Ellesse and Speedo – the iconic performance swimwear brand.

We met a chap called Tim Wright, then licensing manager for Pentland, at their swish North London offices. We talked about licensing one of their brands, eventually selecting Speedo. With the Olympic Games coming up in 2004 and Speedo having over $1 billion in sales, we thought developing a range of performance toiletries for them was a no-brainer.

Wrong.

As good as the Speedo brand was, translating it into performance shampoos, conditioners and skincare products for men and women was much tougher in practice. When we launched the products in 2002 into Boots, Tesco, Superdrug and Sainsbury's, we found we had a big problem – no one bought them. I guess, in hindsight, people were pretty happy with the shampoo or conditioner they bought as part of their weekly shop. Our products, which had a USP of Hydro-creatine™ – a hair-strengthening additive – failed to find resonance with the consumer. With sales in the low thousands and a spiralling marketing budget, we realized we'd made a mistake.

Getting things wrong is part of a healthy business. No one is right all the time – that is a physical impossibility. If you only ever experience 'right', then when 'wrong' rears its troublesome head you won't know how to deal with it.

With Speedo, we had a multi-year contract with some pretty aggressive minimum sales targets. So, Herbie and I found ourselves with a major problem. In our tenth year of business two brands were doing really well, King of Shaves and Ted Baker; Fish was growing slowly, but the losses we were suffering with Speedo were dragging the company down. We knew we needed to act, and fast, to head off impending disaster, so scheduled a meeting with Tim at Pentland. (Tim has since left – he now works with me as sales and marketing director for King of Shaves!)

Hoping we'd be let off gently, we quickly found out that Pentland is a business, and businesses exist to make money. If we wanted out of our agreement, it was going to cost us, big time.

Reeling a bit from the meeting, Herbie and I realized we'd have to sort this out quickly. We were able to negotiate a period in which to pay off our contractual obligation and at the same time explained to some of our long-term suppliers that things were going to be tight for a good few months. In fact, the timing really couldn't have been worse. We hosted a ten-year celebration aboard a motor yacht in the Solent in spring 2003, to which we invited all our key suppliers and retail partners. Within weeks we had to explain to them all that payment terms would have to be pushed out to nearly ninety days.

A lesson learnt

It was a bittersweet time for me. I felt that I'd let the arrogance of complacency slip in. As CEO, it was ultimately my decision what our business did, which brands we handled and how we could continue to grow successfully. Sales were now about £6 million and still climbing, but profitability was going to be hammered.

'Never again,' I said to myself, making a mental note to never do something that could capsize and sink the business I'd founded. So, if the arrogance of complacency rears its head – the belief that you'll always be right, always do well and that you don't have to worry about failure – make sure you knock it on the head straightaway.

Chapter 14: The King of Blades

Taking on *two* 800-pound gorillas

The two questions I was most often asked around this time were 'Will you sell to Gillette?' and 'When are you doing a King of Shaves razor?' With regard to the first question, my answer would be 'Unlikely' and to the second 'Wait and see . . .'

Back in 2001 I'd registered a number of trademarks, including King of Blades. When this was published as a registered trademark, I recall taking a call from a journalist at *Marketing Week*, who asked what my intentions were with regard to razors. Were we taking on Gillette? Would there be a battle of the blades? 'Watch this space,' I said.

Gillette and Schick-Wilkinson Sword are the twin 800-pound gorillas in razors and blades. In fact, I've described Gillette as an 8,000-pound gorilla, so dominant is it in the hardware (razors and blades) sector. Founded in the late nineteeth century, Gillette grew to be the Goliath of shaving. Gillette patented the safety razor, whereby a consumer bought a handle (or was given one) that needed replacement blades. In time, the Gillette business model became a Harvard Business School case study. The business grew slowly at first, but with increasing momentum, and when Gillette razors were supplied to service personnel in both world wars, the business transformed. If you didn't want a beard, you had to shave. And if you chose to shave, the best choice was Gillette.

The founder himself died penniless, but the business continued to grow, to the extent that in 2005 it was bought by US consumer-goods leviathan Procter & Gamble (P&G) for $57 billion dollars. A staggering amount.

Gillette's only global competitor, Schick-Wilkinson Sword, was created by the merger of Schick (founded by Colonel Schick) and the UK sword-to-razor maker Wilkinson Sword. Owned by Warner-Lambert during the 1990s, when Pfizer, a major pharmaceutical company, took over Warner-Lambert they decided Schick-Wilkinson Sword was a non-core business and decided to sell it. Schick-Wilkinson Sword was bought by Energizer Battery, Inc. of St Louis in January 2004 for $930 million.

In 1998 Gillette launched the Mach3, the world's first triple-bladed razor. It employed a number of clever innovations, making it undoubtedly the world's best system razor. Catching the zeitgeist of men's grooming and by using aggressive marketing, sales of Mach3 literally went through the sound barrier. In just seven years over 360 million handles and 6 billion cartridges were sold, making it one of the most successful product launches of all time.

Schick-Wilkinson Sword countered with their Quattro in 2004 and for a while were engaged in patent infringement suits with Gillette, until they settled their differences out of court. Claim and counterclaim was made about the 'closeness' of the shave, the 'comfort' and more.

Stung by Schick-Wilkinson Sword introducing a four-bladed razor, Gillette introduced the five-bladed Fusion in 2005, backed by a simply enormous (hundreds and hundreds of millions of dollars) marketing spend At the time of writing, this is the state of play. Gillette is *fifty-seven* times bigger than Schick-Wilkinson Sword, itself a $1-billion company.

There's money in them there razors and blades . . .

That's why there are approximately 20,000 patents filed by Gillette and Schick-Wilkinson Sword. The razor and blade business model is so successful that it's been adopted by inkjet printer manufacturers (ever wonder why the printer is so cheap yet the replacement cartridges so expensive?) and even coffee brands like Nespresso (buy the machine and get the replacement capsules only online, at prices set by Nespresso).

Disrupting the market

The razor and blades business is no mug's game, but I intended to disrupt it; to challenge the somewhat cosy duopoly enjoyed by Gillette and Schick-Wilkinson Sword, both huge brands and both seemingly impossible to dislodge.

Their size didn't faze me. After all, back in 1993 I'd brought out a 'zag' product that provided very stiff competition to Wilkinson Sword's shaving software products, and had managed to fight off competition from brands like Nivea for Men and L'Oréal Men Expert.

Shaving looks like a pretty simple business. You sharpen a blade, drag it down your skin and the hair falls away. You couldn't make it any simpler, right? Wrong. There's a huge amount of engineering technology in manufacturing a razor blade that has the highest quality, the sharpest edge and, most importantly, cuts the hair without cutting the skin. Over the years shaving companies have invested hundreds of millions of pounds in research and development (R&D) into making tens of billions of razor blades, all exactly the same, with the same razor-sharp qualities. To find out what a dodgy razor blade feels like you only have to buy 'genuine' replacement cartridges online, often made in China, which look like the real thing but on your first stroke you'll find they aren't.

As our ten-year anniversary approached, I started to think more and more about the King of Shaves razor. What would it look like? How would it be different, yet better? How could I break into and disrupt a global duopoly? How could I compete against multimillion pound advertising spends? Why would anyone choose our razor over the self-proclaimed 'Best a man can get'?

The iPod of the shaving market

Designing and launching the King of Shaves Azor took five years – five long years of research, investigation and many meetings with multiple potential partners. We had to think out of the box in terms of the razor's look, feel and patent potential. We constantly examined the competition's products during the period of gestation, with both Gillette and Wilkinson Sword launching new models. Three objectives were prevalent in my mind:

- Simplicity
- Performance
- Affordability

I saw that the razor had been getting increasingly expensive and complicated. Batteries had been added (Mach3 Power, Quattro Energy) simply because Gillette owned Duracell and Energizer owned Wilkinson Sword. I really couldn't see the advantage of a vibrating razor. It seemed to me a cunning way to simply sell more batteries, and in doing so reduce the number of blades offered with each handle.

The cost of shaving was going through the roof. With the introduction of Fusion, Gillette started charging the consumer up to £2 per individual cartridge, and where the Fusion Power cartridge was concerned, up to £2.50. That meant a pack of eight blades was nearly £20! As far as I was concerned, the competition weren't following a 'same, but better' strategy. The marketers were in the driving seat and they were selling a 'same, marginally better, but *far more expensive*' product. It looked like Gillette and Wilkinson Sword were following the dangerous path taken by the US computer giants of the 1980s – IBM and DEC. They made their computers with ever-more disk space, ever-more processing power and ever-more unnecessary features, and, critically, they became ever-more expensive.

During this time I'd been watching the growth of the iPod with interest. Herbie had bought himself one in 2001 and it was certainly an elegant, 'decomplexified' piece of kit. The iPod played MP3s with a style and finesse that simply blew away competitors like the Sony Walkman. Indeed, today there are over 25,000 MP3-playing products, but one brand stands head and shoulders above the rest – the iPod.

I decided I had to develop the iPod of razors. Beautifully designed and superbly engineered, our razor would be the embodiment of shaving simplicity; sleek, elegant and stylish, everything, in my opinion, that my competitors' razors were not.

Project Tomahawk

In early 2003 I sat down with an industrial designer, James Mason, and laid out my thinking for the King of Shaves Azor (although the razor was not actually named until early in 2008, see page 278). I explained that there were literally hundreds of patents out there we had to avoid; from how the cartridge fitted into the head, the alignment of the blades, how to incorporate a skin-tensioning bumper that allows a closer shave and many, many more problems we had to solve. I knew what I wanted our razor to look like and initially worked with some designers from Bucks Technology College in High Wycombe. By August we'd designed a (non-working) proto-type, which had been made into a model.

It looked unique. Slim, and with curves, it had a 'wishbone' or 'pitchfork' head, which allowed the cartridge to be attached by simply pressing inwards. The cartridge utilized blades that curved (which we patented) and it was designed to be manufactured with as little energy consumption and material wastage as possible.

Even the packaging was what I term Ecoptimised®; designed to be minimal, yet as functional and ergonomically pleasing as possible. I'd written literally pages to myself about the King of Blades razor. How I would market it. What its performance would be like. What price we'd charge. In mid-2003 I hired a friend of mine, Martin Park, then a project manager at the software company Oracle, to work with me on pulling all the detail together. This detail was put into the 'Project Tomahawk' folder; it contained all our findings, research and notes. It was a big project, sophisticated and complex.

The design of the razor handle and patents surrounding it was only half of the problem. The other was the cartridge, and more importantly, finding a partner to work with to develop a razor cartridge that would compare favourably with, or possibly be better than, the competitors'. This literally took years. Four years, in fact. Clearly, Gillette were a no-go area and after discussions with Schick-Wilkinson Sword, we realized they didn't want to work with us either. That left a small handful of companies in the world that we could develop the King of Blades with – some based in South East Asia, some in Europe and one in the US. Martin and I met all of them and all seemed unable or unwilling to work with us.

In the spring 2004 though, I had a breakthrough, although it was over two years before it became a reality. I'd met with Mr Koji Endo, President of Kai, a Japanese technology company, through another contact I'll refer to for confidentiality reasons as 'A'. At that stage it looked an impossible task to develop a cartridge that would work in concert with our unique handle, but the breakthrough did come. Meanwhile, in the autumn of 2004, I visited our US office and called a guy who had recently set up a company to sell private-label razors (e.g. supermarket own brand) in the US.

He took my call and we arranged to meet at his home in Los Angeles in October. I flew there, extremely excited, and over afternoon drinks took him through my strategy for a King of Blades razor. The fact he was hosting me at his home felt good and we signed a non-disclosure agreement. We ate at one of my favourite restaurants, Matsuhisa (the original Nobu), in Beverly Hills that night and were joined by a chap I'd met in Miami the previous year, Scott Shiffman, who for many years was executive producer of the huge global TV hit, *CSI: Miami.*

Returning to the UK, I told Herbie and Martin about the meeting and was met, it's fair to say, with quite a bit of scepticism. Put simply, there were one or two razor and blade partners we could work with and had been talking to, and the chances of getting a strong partnership together looked remote. I hadn't returned with anything other than a 'Leave it with me' and I guess I took my contact's words at face value. It turned out that Herbie's scepticism was well placed, as the meeting came to nothing.

In spring 2005 it was announced that P&G were buying Gillette and I knew that our chances of competing in a meaningful way were now even slimmer. P&G is renowned as one of the best consumer product marketing companies in the world, headquartered in Cincinnati, Ohio and run by A. G. Lafley, a master marketer. With Gillette announcing the launch of Fusion, things were clearly hotting up in the hardware market.

I was 100 per cent immersed in Project Tomahawk. The company was continuing to grow nicely and we were all busy. Andy Hill had been promoted to managing director and was starting to build his own team around him. Herbie was increasingly working on Ted Baker and our licensed products business, looking for businesses or brands to acquire. He and I had moved out of the main KMI office into a separate office, where I could sit alongside Martin to work away on the myriad issues we faced.

One thing I was clear about with our razor was as much of it as possible would be manufactured in the UK. Amazingly, Chesham (where King of Shaves is headquartered) turned out to be a bit of a hotbed of razor-tooling companies and potential manufacturers. In 2005 we met potential partners who were willing to tool up our handle (a major project in itself, costing hundreds of thousands of pounds) and physically make it. I was also keen that all the packaging was sourced within a 30-mile radius of KMI and I wanted a slimline approach in contrast to our over-packaged competitors.

We were now filing for patent protection for our razor's features and benefits, with one of its key features being a bendy head. Rather than using a conventional pivot or swivel mechanism, mechanical in function and with plenty of patents out there protecting it, I'd spent ages thinking to myself how our razor could achieve a similar function, but in a simpler way.

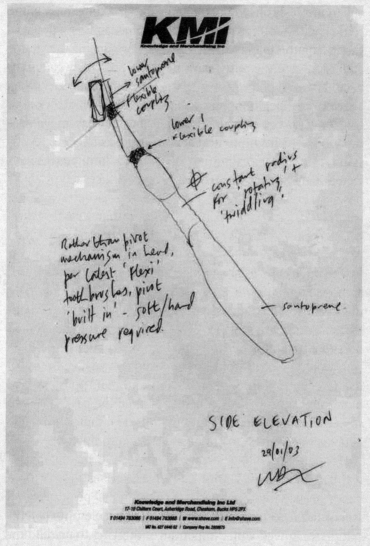

KMi
Knowledge and Merchandising Inc

lower
santoprene
flexible
coupling

lower
flexible coupling

constant radius
for 'rotating',
'twiddling'.

Rather than pivot
mechanism in head,
per Colest 'Flexi'
toothbrushes, pivot
'built in' - soft/hard
pressure required.

santoprene

SIDE ELEVATION

29/01/03

Knowledge and Merchandising Inc Ltd
17-19 Chiltern Court, Asheridge Road, Chesham, Bucks HP5 2PX
T 01494 783066 / F 01494 783055 / W www.shave.com / E info@shave.com
VAT No. 627 0440 92 / Company Reg No. 289875

In early 2003 while brushing my teeth at home I looked at my flexible-headed toothbrush and thought 'We could achieve a similar function with a razor!' The next day, I asked Andy to cut

253

the toothbrush's head in half and superglue a cartridge on to it so I could shave with it. The results were pleasing – the head flexed comfortably and as I pressed down harder on it the rubber resisted the push, allowing me to accurately gauge the right amount of pressure. Often, pushing too hard when shaving causes razor burn while the swivel/pivot systems employed by our competitors often let the head move back too easily. The solution that we eventually developed from my initial idea, incorporating our Bendology®Technology hinge, sought to address this.

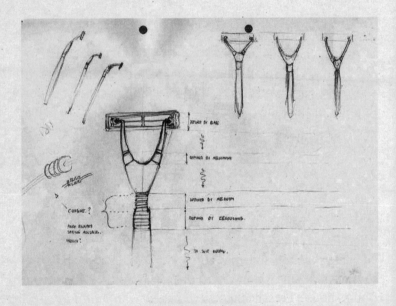

It took a further year or so for the patent to be granted on the hinge, along with other important protections regarding the loading and unloading of the cartridge and the overall look of the razor. During this time Herbie continued to be supportive of my project. Clearly it was consuming cash at quite a rate and there was no guarantee that we'd ever launch the razor, especially as we were still to find a quality blade to fit it. We'd worked with one potential partner to launch a razor called The RZR with Boots in 2005. However, this hadn't sold well, as it employed the conventional stacked-blade technology rather than the more advanced (and hugely patented) open-blade architecture. Wilkinson Sword had stacked blades (which clogged) but had managed to get around that problem by opening the gaps between the blades and wrapping them in thin wire. This looked clumsy to me and was a route I didn't intend to follow.

Who is John Terry?

Although I was totally immersed in developing a razor to 'shave the world' with, I was still dialled into marketing opportunities for the King of Shaves brand. In November 2005, just before sailing across the Atlantic Ocean in an Oyster 53, a fortieth-birthday treat to myself, I'd taken a call from a chap calling from Peter Kenyon's office at Chelsea FC asking whether we would be interested in talking to Chelsea about signing an endorsement deal with John Terry.

Now, football isn't my passion and I didn't actually know who 'JT' was, but I was flattered to receive the call and said that I'd get back in touch with them. I completely forgot about the conversation, until, after returning from sailing the Atlantic, at Doug's house, I recalled it. 'Do you know who John Terry is?' I asked Doug.

Doug stared at me, slightly incredulously, and said, 'He's the Chelsea skipper and England defender. He might even be the next England captain after next year's World Cup. Why do you ask?'

'Well, apparently he wants to do an endorsement deal with King of Shaves.'

Taken aback, Doug exclaimed, 'Well, you'd better meet him then!'

Having had Will Carling on our books in the mid-1990s, I knew the power of marrying brand with sports celebrity but thought there was no way we'd be able to make the financials works. Coincidentally, my son Cameron went to school with footballer Dennis Wise's son, Henry, near Beaconsfield. I didn't really know Dennis, but one day I happened to be outside the school as he was dropping off Henry. 'Hi, my name's Will, I own King of Shaves, the shaving brand. Can I just ask you a quick question?'

'Sure,' Dennis answered.

'Well, before I went away prior to Christmas, I took a call from someone from Chelsea, asking if I was interested in doing a brand endorsement with John Terry. Do you know him, by any chance?'

'Of course. I was at Chelsea while he was working his way up through the youth team. Even better, I'm good friends with his agent, Aaron. Tell you what, I'll give him a call now.'

Slightly flabbergasted, I watched as Dennis called up Aaron, exchanged a few words, then passed the phone to me. 'Hi, this is Will King, founder of King of Shaves. I understand that John is interested in signing a brand endorsement deal with us?'

'Well, I'm not too sure,' Aaron said. 'Who told you?'

'I took a call from Peter Kenyon's office before Christmas,' I replied.

'I'll get back to you,' Aaron said, and hung up.

I handed back Dennis's mobile. 'Good luck,' he said. 'Let me know if I can do anything else for you.'

It transpired that we needed the approval of both Chelsea

FC and John's agent to sign a deal with him. Over the first few months of 2006 we had quite a few meetings in London, culminating with a final one held with John at Stamford Bridge after one of Chelsea's training sessions. We all sat in a large room to discuss what our plans were to use John Terry in our first TV ad campaign, which was due to air before the World Cup.

I knew that aligning a brand with a person had its risks, but also knew if we could agree a deal it would put us in the same division as Gillette, who'd had Beckham on their books. 'It's like a Vauxhall Conference team playing in the Premier League and winning,' I thought to myself as we discussed the contractual points. Nathan Pillai, one of the guys who had brokered the deal with us on behalf of Chelsea FC said, 'John will bring stature to King of Shaves, Will. He's a leader, a world-class footballer and could well be the next captain of England. I suggest you agree the deal.'

We agreed the deal. We ran a TV ad ('Be the best you can be – be a king') on ITV and Sky and made the most of our Premier League signing. England were knocked out of the World Cup and before I knew it John Terry had been installed as England skipper. I heard the news while having lunch with my dad and my girlfriend, (I'd separated from my wife in spring 2004) at J Sheekey. Amazingly, Steven Gerrard's agent, Jon Holmes, was in the restaurant (the same Jon Holmes I'd done the Will Carling deal with eleven years earlier) and he congratulated me that 'the best man got it'. For about ten minutes I was in shock as I thought Stevie G had secured the captaincy, but was soon bombarded with texts and e-mails when it was announced that John Terry was the new England captain.

We've done deals with a number of sportspeople. In September 2004 we signed a deal with Kristan Bromley, aka Dr

Ice, who was due to compete in the skeleton event (sliding headfirst down a bobsleigh track on a small sled) in the forthcoming Winter Olympics, to be held in Turin in February 2006. In April 2005 we held a press conference and had some good publicity, and in December launched the first of our online advergames – KingofSkeleton.com – featuring Kristan sliding down a bobsleigh track..The prize was to accompany us to watch Kristan in the Olympics. Early in 2006 he got some fantastic publicity branded up in our King of Shaves race suit, and we were excited about sponsoring a potential medallist.

Opportunity knocked again. Out of the blue, Kristan called me just before leaving to go out to Turin. 'Will, Kristan here. Look, this is a big favour, but my girlfriend Shelley Rudman is also sliding in the Olympics and doesn't have a sponsor. Is there any chance you might consider sponsoring her?'

I asked, 'How much?'

'Will, whatever you can afford. I know your budgets are tight but seriously, anything would make a difference to her. Can I ask her to call you?'

Having rung off, I immediately called Brian MacLaurin to ask his view from a publicity perspective. 'Will, I can't say yes because to be honest, I've never heard of her. But, it's your decision.'

Two is better than one, I thought to myself. I called Kristan back, said we'd work something out and that I'd put my designers in touch to get some logos sorted out. Brian quickly pulled together a press release: 'King of Shaves to sponsor Olympic sliders, Shelley and Kristan' and got it out to the media.

I guess we've got quite a history of backing 'challengers to winners' in sport. As well as signing Will Carling, we also had another lucky break in 2001, when Herbie took a call from Jo, who worked distributing King of Shaves for us. 'Herbie, I know you like powerboating [Herbie had recently bought a 40-foot powerboat]. Do you think King of Shaves would be interested in backing Neil [her husband] in the Honda F4 Powerboat Championships?'

'You'd better speak to Will,' he said.

Upon speaking with Jo, I found out that the driver was to be a chap called James Sheppard, who was funding the project (i.e. buying the powerboat, dealing with the running costs, etc.) but he wanted a 'cool brand' to be title sponsor.

'How much?' I asked.

'Speak to Neil,' she said.

Within a week or so we'd agreed a very reasonable price for King of Shaves to sponsor James and Neil in offshore powerboat racing'.

Neither Herbie nor I had particularly high hopes for much media coverage, but boy, were we amazed. Not only did James and Neil dominate that season, winning the championship convincingly, but midway through the series Channel 4 announced they would be covering it, with further coverage on Sky Sports. It was literally the Honda and King of Shaves Powerboat Show! Winning almost every race meant we got tons of press coverage, even a feature in the *Sunday Times*, which coincided neatly with a business article on Herbie and me.

The awareness for King of Shaves, both at the events and via TV and press, was worth many times what I'd paid James and Neil, so at the F4 Powerboat awards held at the Hilton Heathrow, I agreed to sponsor them for a further two years. I wrote the details on the back of a paper napkin. It was a great evening. I increased the sponsorship quite a bit, feeling that the coverage we'd had had been outstanding. In addition, I said if James ever got a P1 or C1 ride (the powerboat equivalent of Formula 1) and King of Shaves was in a position to sponsor him, then we would.

Over the next three years the King of Shaves-backed team dominated the Honda Series in the UK, winning their class four times in a row. James went on to drive in C1 catamarans, powered by twin Lamborghini V12 engines (spectacularly crashing at 140 miles per hour at the Plymouth Grand Prix, a really 'close shave') and finally won P1, the monohull World Championship in 2007.

With our successful sponsorship of powerboating, skeleton (Shelley Rudman nailed a silver medal in Turin and she and Kristan were briefly household names) and our Young Blades sports bursary programme (we have up to twelve aspiring sportsmen and women as part of our grass roots commitment to sports), I thought to myself, 'Why not football?' And so followed the deal with John Terry.

In addition to KingofSkeleton.com, we further leveraged the signings of James and Neil and John Terry with advergames. All were designed and produced by Chris Kemp – Salt of Kempt Ltd, a leading online viral game design company. All can be found at kingofgames.co.uk. To date we have had well over 100 million players, with the John Terry game, King of Defenders, having had over 50 million plays alone.

These signings, all world class, were in my opinion incredibly important in continually leveraging the influence and appearance of King of Shaves as a global brand. In the US in 2003, we'd signed Jason Kidd, a top NBA star who played for the New Jersey Nets, to endorse King of Shaves, and now Google was starting to dominate internet search, it didn't take long to see that King of Shaves punched way above its weight in brand leverage and endorsement.

Secret meeting

In November 2006 I took a call from 'A', the guy I'd first met in February 2004, who said, 'Meet me in London. I'm staying at the Portman Intercontinental. I have something that will interest you.' He flew in the next morning and I raced into town, meeting him at about 8.30 a.m. in his hotel room. I'd told no one at KMI. I wanted to see what he had. Slightly conspiratorially he said, 'I have what you're looking for. Have a shave with it and tell me what you think.' I gingerly took a bubble-wrapped razor handle from him and opened it. 'Don't worry about the handle,' he said, 'just let me know what you think of the shave.'

I had deliberately not shaved, so pulled off my shirt, massaged in some shaving oil and shaved. It was excellent. Not only did the cartridge deliver a close, comfortable shave, but the cartridge architecture allowed great wash-through after shaving – what is termed a Wash Through Index® – a trademark we own, incidentally. The razor had been developed by our 'cutting edge' technology partner Kai.

'It's great!' I said. 'I need to get Herbie to have a shave with it. I'll call him now.' It was still before 9 a.m. I got hold of Herbie and told him to get to Portman Square to have a shave. He had yet to leave his house, but by 10.15 a.m. he was in the hotel bedroom with 'A' and me. He washed the cartridge thoroughly – we only had the one – and had a shave. 'Seems good,' he said, 'nice and close. So, what's the next step?'

We talked at length about the development process and the fact that it could be up to another two years before we would be able to put a King of Blades cartridge on a King of Blades handle. That would be November 2008. Talk about a marathon. I explained to 'A' that we really needed to speed things up. Our competitors would almost certainly have new products out by then and another two years was simply too long. 'I'll see what I can do,' he said. 'Leave it to me.'

Chapter 15: Launching the Azor

If you haven't read about Chinese warlord Sun Tzu, and how he went about winning battles, then get a copy of *The Art of War* and immerse yourself. It's fascinating stuff. The campaigns he conducted make for instructive reading, particularly if you're considering taking on global behemoths. In short, Sun Tzu writes that 'A battle is already won, before it is fought' and that engaging in wargames – working out what your enemy is going to do, with what and when – is an investment worth making.

The battle plan

I needed to find someone to work with me to develop the launch strategy for our razor. The strategy had to be one that could survive repeated advertising onslaughts, aggressive trade promotions and more. At the same time as KMI was founded, I came across a chap called Paul Walton, who'd just founded a brand strategy consultancy called The Value Engineers. He'd been an early adopter of the internet and uploaded a paper that somehow I came across and read, and over the years we'd loosely kept in touch. He'd introduced me to a guy who worked at Unilever who had experience of how they'd kept their Lynx (Spray More, Get More) brand at the top of its game. I thought that Paul might know someone who had worked at Gillette or Procter & Gamble who would be prepared to spend a year or so with me working on strategy.

In late 2006, Paul and I had a meeting and he offered to try and come up with some names. One chap we met had worked for Unilever when Lynx had launched their ill-fated 3 Blade Shave razor but we didn't take him on. Paul then recommended another woman, Ms B, who had a strong background in fast moving consumer goods (FMCG) and had worked extensively across a variety of brand platforms in concert with major retailers. I met her and thought she had a great combination of confidence, common sense and ability. Within a few weeks we'd hired her as a consultant and, with Martin leaving KMI to return to Oracle, she moved into my office, along with Herbie.

I asked her to immerse herself in King of Shaves, work on a few product development projects for us – our women's line for example – look at the US business and gather her thoughts for some heavy discussion with me.

Having not seen the cartridge, she was sceptical about our ability to challenge a well-established duopoly and repeatedly made the point that 'The competition is going to come at you all guns blazing'. I thought, 'Well, that means they're going to throw money at trying to solve the problem – out-promote us, out-advertise us and try to smother us.' Having never had access to major money this didn't worry me in the slightest. What concerned me more was convincing the sceptical UK retailers about our launch and how it would be great news for their consumers, for them and, of course, for us. A triple whammy if ever there was one.

Potential investors

As the global boom in the first half of 2007 continued unabated, I was heavily distracted by potential deals with private equity companies. Knowing we'd need quite a lot of money, certainly in the millions to successfully launch the razor and deal with its working capital requirements, we were regularly meeting potential investment partners. More often than not the investment partners and directors of these companies displayed an unnerving level of arrogance. They were awash with cash provided by ever-speculative investors – banks, hedge funds and high net-worth individuals – and the deals that were being done were increasingly dependent on heavy borrowing. Indeed, one of the largest deals done during 2007 was when Stefano Pessina and Kohlberg Kravis Roberts & Co. (KKR), the US private equity firm, took Boots PLC private, with billions and billions of pounds of debt loaded on to the balance sheet.

I didn't like the look of these companies one tiny bit. Indeed, as I sit here two years on, a lot of them have suffered hugely, with their investments being bankrupted under the load of debt or they have been hit by the realization that their business model simply wasn't viable. I've always loved the fact that King of Shaves is a belt and braces business, selling millions of individual units, each on a decent margin, to millions of consumers. It's a very risk-averse business, which maybe appeared dull in the heady pre-downturn days of 2006 and early 2007, but now people view the business in a far more positive way.

Over the years Herbie and I have had many approaches regarding either investing in or buying King of Shaves, but for one reason or another none of them made sense. In my mind we were yet to do our 'big thing' and potential investors could never get their heads around the value we placed on the business – a healthy multiple of sales. I guess it was because no one truly believed we could compete against our global competitors and make serious inroads into their business, but I knew we could.

All systems go

In April, I was sitting in Andy's office when Amy, one of our staff members, came into the room and handed me a FedEx parcel. I didn't know who it was from, so opened it without too much interest. Inside were half a dozen razor cartridges, slightly different from the one I'd shaved with in November 2006, and a note that said fifty more would be with me by the end of the month. I guess it was at this time I realized we were going to launch. Tooling up for razor blades costs a great deal of money and it was clear our partner believed in our market and product proposition, and had made the investment. Now it was time for us to make Project Tomahawk a reality.

Winding back three or so years earlier, in the early stages of the razor discussion I'd met a chap called Andy Honour and his boss, Richard Powell, of a Chesham-based company called Euromoulds. I doubt they expected to see me again, but somehow I knew I'd work with them. Just a three-minute walk away from our office, they specialize in designing sophistica-ted tools that allow 'twin-shot' hybrid plastic and elastomer products to be manufactured. I knew they'd be an ideal partner, especially as I was determined the Azor would be made in the UK. They had a lot of expertise in this area, in fact Andy, the design engineer, had worked on a number of precision projects for Dyson, which reassured me of their ability. I went to their office, showed them our cartridge and said, 'Remember what I showed you a few years ago? Well, we're now in a position to launch. So, how long will it take me to get a handle designed, tooled and manufactured?'

It felt critically important to me to be closely involved in the design of the razor. Its look and feel had been very much my idea, and knowing that Ferraris weren't designed by committees, to maintain its elegant, stylish look I would need to work very much one on one with Andy.

I think Andy would concur when I say that it took a little while for him to trust my vision for the razor and understand that I wouldn't be deflected with compromise or dilution. Although our razor looks very simple, simplicity in design and engineering is often the hardest thing to get right. Our top priority was ensuring that there was a very simple mechanism to load and unload the cartridge. My original idea proved unworkable, so Andy spent months finessing a solution.

As spring turned into summer (when we first pitched our concept to Boots) and summer into autumn, Andy got closer and closer to something that he was happy with that could, first, be tooled (a major investment) and, second, manufactured (an even bigger one). As we worked together we came up with improvements all the time. One such improvement was for the cartridge-release mechanism (which has been further evolved since the launch) and another idea I was particularly pleased with was the integration of the elastomer bumper that 'pre-tensions' the skin prior to the shave into the handle. You only have to look at a Gillette Fusion cartridge, where the bumper is thrown away with the cartridge (what a waste), to realize we were coming up with a genuinely different take on the razor.

Andy takes up the story:

> *As I worked on the design, Will constantly reminded me how he wanted it to work and look, always aiming to get back to the vision he had. The final result is amazingly close to the original concept drawings Will had shown us years before.*

> *Looking back, Will had taken on the management of the project almost alone. While this might seem a rather narrow-minded way to run an important project, he had a vision and impetus to get to the finish line. The involvement of too many people would have highlighted the difficulties and watered down the enthusiasm that he was able to bring to the project. I find it a great compliment and rather frightening the trust Will put in me to pull together the engineering of the Azor. I am sure other companies would have put together a much larger team to get the job done. This would not have produced something as unique and innovative as the Azor, which has reached the market in almost the exact form that Will envisioned five years before.*

I had only shown a prototype razor once to Herbie. It was a dirty-white colour prototype, and to be honest, unless you had a clear idea what the end product would look like, you'd feel pretty uninspired by it. In fact, he was, and we had a pretty heated discussion about it – how much money had been spent, what the result could be. In the end I asked Herbie to trust me that the final product would be fantastic. I'm not sure he believed me, but he gave me the benefit of the doubt.

Making a splash

As autumn 2007 approached, the shock news that Northern Rock was to be nationalized hit the headlines and I had a feeling that things were going to change, and *fast*. Business is all about momentum and the confidence that was keeping the momentum going in the global economy had taken a big knock. So much has happened to reverse the world's economy in such a short period of time, it's almost unbelievable. But, deep down, I felt our timing was right. People would start to eschew 'overpriced and expensive' and start to look at genuine value-for-money alternatives. 'Our razor will deliver the "King of Shaves" without the ransom,' I thought to myself, continually jotting my thoughts down in my ever-present moleskin diary.

I had to get ahead of the game, and had in mind a marketing strategy that could unfurl like a sail, catching the wind and making our yacht (business) go faster. I knew what the initial launch strategy would be. Having read Alistair Campbell's diaries while on holiday I knew I'd run our launch exactly like a general election. We'd be the Fair Shave party, we'd be tough on stubble and the causes of stubble and come down hard on the stealthy shaving taxes being levied by our competitors. For a while, I was even considering relocating my campaign office into Millbank Tower on the Thames, where Labour had fought their successful 1997 general election campaign!

One item I'd decided I definitely did want was a campaign battle bus. I wanted a six wheeler, with blacked-out windows, an upstairs area where we could hold meetings with journalists and our retail partners, and a downstairs area with shaving stations. Having no idea where to find one, I knew a man who would and put in a call to David Green, previously CEO of the United Kingdom Sailing Association (UKSA). I'd first met Dave back in the 1980s when he was a seasonal windsurfing instructor at the NSC. In 2005, David had led the project that raised £1 million to take Sir Francis Chichester's world-girdling yacht, *Gipsy Moth IV*, from a concrete grave in Greenwich, London, back to sailing the seven seas, backed by companies including BT, and of course, King of Shaves. Over the summer of 2007, he'd decided he wanted to run his own consultancy and we came up with the name 3Greenlights (as there is no amber or red where David is concerned). Extremely enthusiastic and renowned for putting the rubber on the road (his words), he would be the ideal guy to be my campaign project manager. It's worth hearing from Dave, as enthusiasm like his is hard to find:

I worked alongside Will for a year, through the heart of the Azor campaign. I have never received so many cryptic e-mails, so many wild ideas or embarked on so many crazy missions but through all of it Will remained focused on the 'big idea' and creating the noise about his product that would put his competitors in the shade. He wanted me to buy a double-decker bus and make it into the 'coolest mobile shaving emporium on earth' so we could move it around the country giving away Azors and introducing shaving neophytes to the ultimate shaving experience. This we did, to some considerable acclaim, and people the length and the breadth of Britain saw the shaving stations and shaving demonstrations, took up the Wii Azor Guitar Hero Game and played the Azor Footie Challenge.

David and I quickly agreed project-management terms, and I put Brian MacLaurin on to a war footing as my media consultant. I reckoned they'd both need to be on contract for about year to get the job done. I also got back together with Peter Cook, whom I'd last worked with at Hedges Wright, to produce the launch events for the razor; it would be launched firstly to my staff and secondly to Boots' senior management. He was now the owner of the highly successful UK production company, Peter Cook Productions, and it was great to work with him once again.

I'd kept the contents of the presentation to the King of Shaves staff a secret. I hoped the event, held at the Soho Hotel in London, would be like a mini party conference. There was a manifesto with our 'four-edged pledge'; my speech, penned by David Block, a talented copy and speechwriter; and more. I'd invited my dad and brother Doug, and for about forty minutes I gave a talk from a lectern, explaining the backstory to King of Shaves, how it had come to be, what we'd achieved so far and what my ambition for the 'King of Blades' was. At the end I'm glad to say there was a solid round of applause and then I took questions from the audience. Dad pulled me aside as people were leaving and whispered, 'Gillette have got a great future behind them!'

It was great having Dad there. Now seventy-five years old, Dad and Mum had invested in the business in the early days. Dad had been able to realize his dream of becoming a pilot in gaining his National Pilot Licence, owning and flying his own light aircraft out of Beccles, near Lowestoft, courtesy of King of Shaves!

The following week we had a similar meeting with two senior Boots executives, who were taken through our market-launch strategy. At this meeting we'd had executives from our partner companies fly in from around the world and, more importantly, Boots were impressed. At the time, we were a regional finalist in the HBOS-sponsored *The Sunday Times* Entrepreneur of the Year Award. As it happened, we were beaten into second place but to be honest it was a huge relief that we could continue our strong banking relationship with HSBC rather than shifting to HBOS, which we'd have been obliged to do if we'd won. In the light of what's happened in the past twelve months, King of Shaves continues to be a company that has somehow got the timing just right.

The moment of truth approaches

The great irony was that at this point I was yet to actually shave with a King of Shaves razor. All I'd shaved with was a cartridge attached to another handle. The manufacture of the tool to actually make the razor was well underway but even at the Boots presentation all I had to show the senior executives was a computer-graphics animation of how our razor's bendy head delivered a close, comfortable shave, how from the front it looked like an Aston Martin DB9 car and how, once it had been launched in black and white, we could do a 'Swatch' with it and make it in any colour our designers cared to come up with.

As 2007 drew to a close I spent more and more time worrying about the finished item. What sort of shave would it deliver? Would the cartridge mechanism work? Would people 'get' it? Could it be a razor of choice against the established competition?

Christmas and New Year passed in a blur. I was pretty distracted with events – KMI had posted a very decent profit and I knew from my industry contacts that there was a buzz that we were up to something. I'd met a senior Procter &

Gamble executive at my brother's Christmas cocktail party. 'They know you're up to something,' she said. 'Don't underestimate the competition, Will.' I had more than a healthy paranoia that somehow news would leak that we were launching a razor when I was working with Brian to plan the media around it meticulously; it was just like Alistair Campbell working with Tony Blair on a major policy announcement.

In early January I started to blog about the fact that we were up to something. King of Shaves has always enjoyed a fantastic online following, as well as great brand loyalty, to the extent that on one occasion, when we were unhappy with a promotional implementation, we e-mailed our database and asked them to 'Pop into— and check our promotion is running.' Over 4,000 people e-mailed us back, some with photos, showing it wasn't and we were able to use this to get a better deal in the next negotiation. I'd chosen Tomahawk as the project name and rejigged this to WKoHAMAT, adding 08 (as it was now 2008), bought the domain name wkohamat08. com and planted this as a banner in our advergame, kingofdefenders.com, on a placard that one of the crowd is holding (I'm pretty sure it's still there). I also started to refer to the fact that 'WKoHAMAT is coming. Click here' and this took people to a site where they could sign up for more information.

In this way we were able to make about 10,000 people aware of our launch in the critical build-up months and start the word of mouth going. I'd taken inspiration from the promotion of the film *Cloverfield*, which used similar techniques to grow awareness without giving away the plot.

I was due to go away sailing to the Windward Islands with my girlfriend in January and was desperate to have shaved with our razor before then. However, Andy wasn't the sort of guy you pushed. I'd learnt to respect how hard and intelligently he worked. He knew more than anyone what the deadlines to launch were (we'd involved him in all our key meetings, even with Boots) and I knew he'd only let me have a scrape when he was happy.

The big moment arrived. 'Will, you might like to have a shave with this. It's not quite right yet, but it's nearly there.'

I grabbed the razor from his hand and looked at it. 'Are you happy with it?' I asked.

'Yes, I think it's elegant, Will. It's come out better than I thought and this is just a first-off.'

Obviously, I'd shaved already that morning but nonetheless wondered what a shave would be like. 'Grab your camera, Andy,' I said, 'I want to get the first King of Shaves scrape on video!'

To my delight it worked exactly as I'd hoped. The razor's flexing head followed the contours first of my cheeks, then my chin and I then changed direction to shave upwards with the grain and, amazingly, there was a bit of growth coming off.

'Bye, bye Mach3,' I thought as I shaved, 'hello King of Blades!' I don't know what Andy made of it, videoing me with his camera. I'm sure he must have thought, 'There's no way our competitors go about developing a razor in this way.' We uploaded the footage on to our server.

I loved the new razor:

1. It worked
2. It looked different
3. All my hard work over the past five years had resulted in a physical product
4. Best of all, I could shave with my own razor

It was like 1993 all over again, not better as such but hugely satisfying. 'Game on,' I thought.

Shaving out of this world

Prior to our ten-day sailing trip in the Windward Islands, I flew to New York to attend a press reception for the formal launch of Virgin Galactic – the spaceship company that Richard Branson founded in 2004 to make 'Affordable space travel a reality'. A lot of people have derided Galactic, downgrading it to space tourism, but what most people don't get is what investments like this bring to areas such as engineering and design, with the philosophy of doing things differently. For example, a conventional rocket is ground-launched, where gravity is strongest and therefore the most energy is required to achieve lift-off. What Virgin Galactic utilized was an air-launched spaceship, slung beneath a mothership (named Eve, after Richard's mum) already 60,000 feet up. As it happened, a chap called Stephen Attenborough had called me in November 2004 and been put through to me on the basis that he was Sir Richard's astronaut relations officer and would I like to be the first to shave in space? How could I say no? 'As long as I get to shave Richard's beard as well,' I laughed.

Taking this 'zag' approach is a great way to differentiate your product. As we sailed around the Windward Islands my thoughts continually turned back to giving our razor brand 'zag'.

Dropping the 'r' in razor

Our razor was still unnamed. Everyone at KMI assumed the razor would be called King of Blades. After all, we owned the trademark and the existing logo could be easily adapted. But I believed it was critical not to diffuse King of Shaves with King of Blades. I'd been thinking about really memorable, successful brand names – Coke, Nike, Puma, Visa, Apple, Mach3, Fusion – and all had between four and six letters in their primary name.

What could the King of Shaves razor be called? iRazor? iShave? I thought back to our test product, the RZR, which now seemed a little contrived. Our razor had four blades, I had designed it to be made 'With less, to deliver more', so why not drop the 'r' and call it Azor? And that was it. We filed Azor in Class 8 with the UK Patent Office and hoped it would get registration. There were no similar marks, so my hopes were high.

Previously I explained that had I gone with Sunrise as the brand name for the men's shaving oil I doubt I would be writing this book now. I needed to feel the same about the name for the King of Shaves razor. It had to last for many years. Of course we'd continue to evolve, improve and hopefully reduce the cost of the razor as sales increased, but unlike our competitors, releasing new handles and cartridges every five years or so wasn't in my game plan.

For me, encouraging and developing innovation and the talent behind it is an area of the economy that needs as much help as possible. The TV show *Dragons' Den*, for example, is about innovation on a superficial level, but is also as much about the interplay between the celebrity investors as it is the potential, or in some cases, actual business talent being showcased. I'm sure if I'd pitched King of Shaves to the dragons, they'd have taken one look at the competition in the market and given the product a low chance of success. However, if I'd had the opportunity to explain to a government-backed panel of investors the strategy, the process and the fact that I only had two genuine competitors, perhaps the business would have been viewed as a realistic long-term investment and perhaps taken less time to achieve the success it has.

Chapter 16: Creating Market Disruption

During a visit to my favourite local gastropub, The Furrow, in Winchmore Hill, I fell into a discussion with the young owner, Sam Clarke, who was also a talented skydiver and base jumper. He'd joked that it'd be 'Fun to do a shave with a guy in a barber's chair, hurtling towards the ground at a hundred miles per hour featuring the new Azor'. Of course we jumped at the chance of such great promotion and a video of the resultant jump can be found on YouTube. Early April saw me at Speakers' Corner launching the King of Shaves Fair Shave party. We shot a short video filmed by cutting between me, my team and a megaphone, and crowds who were gathered near Buckingham Palace. The end result can also be seen on YouTube.

As well as these videos, Gavin Newsham, a freelance journalist, wanted to create an eZine called K.O. (for King Of) and we bought the domain kingofmags.com to host it. This has been a great success and the format is being increasingly adopted by all manner of brands and individuals, including Manchester United and England player Rio Ferdinand!

Launching the Azor

Early May saw our crucial publicity strategy meeting. The scene was set and our twin PR agencies – The Communications Store and Brian MacLaurin Associates [Previously called MacLaurin Communcations] – were briefed. The Communications Store would handle brand PR and Brian MacLaurin Associates would deal with strategy and overall execution. Dave Green's

3Greenlights, our online e-marketing agency Creatormail, advergame specialist Kempt and our media-buying agency John Ayling & Associates all had critical roles to play too. We were on a countdown to the press event, to be held at the stylish Hempel Hotel in West London.

I'd been blogging about our upcoming launch two or three times daily and we had tens of thousands of people signed up to be the first to hear about it. Across men's magazines, such as *FHM*, *Shortlist* and *GQ*, we'd run ads with titles like 'Impossible is Nothing, We're Taking on Gillette' (which resulted in a letter from adidas's lawyers). In the week prior to the launch we ran a double-page spread in *Shortlist*, featuring our King of Shaves AlphaGel and the Azor.

I'd also started running ads across Facebook, the social networking site, with up to fifty ads at any one time, ranging from 'Escape the Matrix' and 'Take the Red Pill' to 'Choose Different, Shave Better'. These were particularly useful and cost-effective to run. We notched up over 100 million ad impressions in the four weeks prior to launch and unlike posters or press ads, it was nearly impossible for the competition to know how many ads we were serving daily and who we were targeting.

One of my young staff members, Matt Bean, was a talented musician and budding rock star, having studied music at Manchester University. In April I'd asked him to see if he could come up with a music track that would refer to 'the folly of five', i.e. cars with five wheels, chairs with five legs, razors with five blades. He did much more than I asked. He created a band called Beanius that played an accomplished set at the launch. Matt also composed the music to the AV presentation. Beanius featured in the King of Air Guitar online game devised by Kempt (1 million players to date and climbing), which went live in July, tying in with the nationwide Azor bus tour.

Press turnout for the launch was fantastic. More than 130 journalists from men's magazines, style bibles, red-tops and broadsheets packed into the downstairs restaurant at the Hempel. As well as the press and retail guests, all the staff were there, as well as other friends, shareholders and my family – Mum, Dad, Doug, Pete and their wives. It was going to be an emotional night, but I was sure, a great one.

And it was. I'd written a speech, but I had second thoughts about it when I got to the venue as it just didn't seem to encapsulate everything that the team and I had achieved, so I took to the lectern and spent twenty-five minutes or so simply explaining what we'd done, how we'd done it and why.

Receiving a fantastic round of applause, I was delighted to see Mum and Dad clapping and smiling, along with Herbie, Doug and everyone else. It's at times like these that you realize how much a team effort contributes towards the vision of one person and I felt incredibly proud and emotional about our achievement. We were the first British razor manufacturer in over 100 years to launch a new razor and with two powerful competitors out there aiming to defend their ground, I knew it would be a battle royal.

I also knew, deep down, that our Azor razor was a great razor. I'd been shaving with the cartridge and then the prototype for over eighteen months and had had a clean, close, comfortable shave every time. The Endurium® coating meant the steel could be sharper and last longer, and with our £4.99 price point for an Azor and three cartridges I knew it was priced for profit, and priced for sale. As no one had one (apart from me) and I believed most people would want to try one, it had the Harvard Rule of Four right at its core (see page 90).

Our strategy for market share was simple – grab five per

cent of the UK market in the first year. We aimed to sell a razor that shaves closer, lasts longer and cost less. There was a huge group of shavers out there either paying too much for their razor or still using ten-year-old technology. We knew we had around a million active customers and felt that if people enjoyed our software then they'd give our hardware a try. To reinforce awareness of the Azor launch (Sainsbury's first, then Boots, to be followed by Tesco and Superdrug in the autumn) we labelled our software with simple 'Try our new razor' stickers.

A great reaction

With *Marketing Week* running a double-page spread about our launch (and with commentators doubting our ability to win even a few percentage points of the market), I knew we were set. One incredibly important interview I'd given prior to the launch was to a *Mail on Sunday* journalist writing for the colour supplement, *Live*. I met him at London restaurant J Sheekey and spent an hour and a half talking to him about the entire project, from start to finish. I'm sure I bored him rigid but the lunch was great and he had a razor review feature coming up, which was due out on Sunday 22 June, the day before the Azor went on sale in Sainsbury's.

I was flying abroad that day and was incredibly nervous about the review. What would it say? How would the Azor fare against Fusion, Quattro and the like? Would the reviewer hate it or love it? Unbiased, independent, quality editorial coverage is the lifeblood of brands. It's the reviewer's opinion and can easily make or break a product. Simply witness the factual coverage by *Horizon*, the science documentary programme, on Boots' No. 7 Protect & Perfect Beauty serum, an anti-ageing product, which sent the sales from just a few thousand a week into the millions!

Picking up the *Mail on Sunday* at the airport, I frantically turned to the piece in *Live* magazine to find that the Azor had . . . a *top* review, four stars, with the comment that 'This is a serious challenger'! The relief I felt was absolutely enormous. I knew not everyone would take to the Azor, but I knew that a positive, authoritative review like that in *Mail on Sunday* would mean that the Azor would at least be trialled by consumers. The coverage continued, with pieces in *Which?* magazine, both in 2008 and 2009, and other independent reviews by magazines like *Shortlist, Esquire, GQ* and even the über-trendy *Wallpaper*. As the plane eased into its nine-hour flight, I fell asleep. Part one, job done. But of course, the job is never done, we're running a brand marathon, remember. On returning to the UK, I boarded the Azor bus as it set off on its tour.

We started the tour at Canary Wharf, linking up with Johnny Vaughan, Lisa Snowdon and Capital FM's Breakfast Show in a charity promotion, 'To Baldly Go', which raised around £40,000 for a cancer-research charity in a single morning. The first stop on the tour was the Lowestoft Airshow.

King of Shaves today

Finally, I'll bring the King of Shaves story right up to date. We've just embarked on a £5 million national advertising campaign designed to make the Azor the number one-selling shaving handle in the UK by the end of 2009. In November 2008 King of Shaves won the prestigious CBI/*Real Business* Company of the Year Award. In February, *Shortlist* awarded it 'Best New Shaving Product' and in March we won *Growing*

Business magazine's and T-Mobile's 'Best Product Company' and overall 'Fast Growth Business 2009'. Bear in mind that the latter award was won during a recession the like of which the UK hasn't seen since 1992.

Now the Azor is launched, we've taken the decision to restructure KMI into twin businesses: The King of Shaves Company Ltd, which will be run by me, reinvesting profits into marketing spend to support our development in the UK and our international market launches in the US, Brazil, Japan, South Africa and Australia; while Herbie will run KMI Brands (which now includes the portfolio of brands owned by Floraroma, acquired by us in 2008) focusing on profitable sales growth, new licence opportunities and mergers and acquisitions.

Will we succeed in my desire to shave the world? Well, if we don't, it won't be for lack of application. There are as many hurdles in our path today as there were back in 1993. But, as ever, I keep my SPACE mantra close to hand, I 'zag' while the competition 'zigs' and always try to be the best I can be. Business success is achievable, accessible, empowering, rewarding and uniquely satisfying. And it's out there. Go get it.

Chapter 17:
Be a Relentless Child

In my final chapter it's time to splice together the individual strands within this book into a coherent strategy for you. 'Splice' is a sailing term. When you splice a rope you join it without using a knot. It's a technique well worth learning if you ever want to put a loop in a rope without losing half its strength, maybe to hook it around a boulder and start rocking it out of its hollow.

Keep the child in you

In my office there's a large poster that hangs opposite my desk that says 'Work Hard and Be Nice To People'. This, in a way, says it all. The harder you work, the luckier you are likely to become and the more satisfaction of success you'll earn. It is said what goes around, comes around. If you work hard and are nice to people, then it's likely the people you work with will return the compliment. Children, before their brains rewire, are generally kindly and collaborative. As adulthood is reached, hatred and competitiveness can rear their head. Hatred may be too strong a word, dislike may be more appropriate, but nonetheless, try and keep the child in you, in the way you operate and interact with other people. It's worked for me, I see no reason why you shouldn't try it.

Partnership

Two is better than one, so go find your Owl. Sure, there are plenty of people who are happy being on their own, but on the whole we're a gregarious lot and enjoy the company of others. In your personal life you'll probably have, or be seeking, a life partner, someone to share your thoughts, experiences and highs and lows with, and this should be no different in your work life. After all, you spend a whole lot of time working. If you're thinking about striking out on your own it's a lot more fun digging the trench for the future foundations of your business with someone else. When the burden gets too heavy, you can take a rest and your partner can take over and keep going. When success starts to rear its head, you have someone to share it with.

SPACE

The SPACE acronym (see page 13) has worked for me and I hope it will set you on the right track. I hope that my story will inspire others to want to start their own business. Some years back a *Sunday Times* journalist called Rachel Bridge wrote a book that summarized the success stories of a handful of entrepreneurs; I was delighted and proud to be featured in it. Fast-forward a few years and at the CBI/*Real Business* Company of the Year Awards I was politely tapped on the shoulder by a couple of young guys from an online start-up company, ASuitThatFits.com. The business was founded by schoolboy friends Warren Bennett and David Hathiramani, who spotted a market niche for mixing technology with their passion for suits, allowing consumers to design their own suit online. Sales are already approaching (or are in) the millions of pounds. Warren said to me, 'Will, I wanted to meet you and thank you because we set up our business after reading about how you'd set up yours in Rachel's book. You inspired us to do it, I just wanted to let you know. Thanks!'

Location, Location, Location

This is as important in the business world as it is when buying a home. Like the saying 'It's the economy, stupid', the only thing that matters where property is concerned is location. In exactly the same way, you must carefully choose in which market you locate your business and through which channels you will make sales. The launch of King of Shaves in Harrods was not a random choice. I was relentless in ensuring Harrods was the first stockist and in making sure Boots stocked us to help us achieve growth in sales volume. Selecting these prime retailers was intrinsic to our success and you need to give the location of your business equally careful consideration.

Same, but better

Coming up with a truly original, never-seen-before product that turns into an outstanding commercial success is probably one of the hardest things to do. Where our Azor is concerned, it's not original but it is, in my opinion, better. Where our competitors' products are expensive, ours are affordable. Where their products are ugly, ours are stylish. Where they spend hundreds of millions of pounds on convincing you to love and buy their products, we try to build genuine satisfaction *into* the DNA of our brand. The day I succumb to launching new products just because we need to keep 'new' on the menu is the day King of Shaves will be on a different trajectory to the one it's on today.

So, embrace new ideas and new pockets of knowledge and information on a daily basis. You can now sort a location for your business by using Google Streetmaps. You can use a web service like Twitter to make people aware of your service or expertise. Meet people, talk about stuff, share experiences – it can make a real difference.

The final word

I'm no celebrity and I have no desire to be one either. I can browse anonymously in Boots in Chesham, Tesco in Amersham, Sainsbury's in Beaconsfield or Waitrose in Marlow, checking that our products are in stock and well-displayed while I'm doing my weekly shop. I can use my common sense to check we are OK on the shelves and if someone is browsing our products I might politely introduce myself as Will King, founder of King of Shaves, and ask if I can answer any questions they might have.

As far as I'm concerned I'm just another person, one who has worked hard (certainly), had a lot of luck (definitely) and was in the right place at the right time to do something worthwhile. My last piece of advice is never knock opportunity. It's rarer than you think and you should never shy away from the chance to challenge yourself, set new goals and move outside your comfort zone. You'll be glad you did.

Best,

Will King
Founder and Chief Shaving Officer, King of Shaves

Index

Note: WK denotes Will King.